Welcome to your Rid

Assessment Page

On the first pages, you can begin to record your current level of overall fitness as a rider. Use the tables to chart your present flexibility, strength, balance, cardiovascular fitness and feeling of stability when riding. Three months later, repeat the process. There are four of these boxes to represent each quarter of a year worth of goal setting and progress.

Riding Skills Goals Worksheet

Use this table to write in your performance goals. Are you trying to learn to sit the trot? Are you looking to post the trot without stirrups? Do you want to be able to jump a specific height of course? Or perhaps ride a cross-country course at a pace for a certain number of minutes?
Think about when and how you will meet those goals. Who will help you and how will you help yourself.

Your Favorites

Record new exercises you'd like to try. Keep track of the ones you enjoy. Exercise is not a punishment for your body. It's a celebration of what it can do. Spend most of your time doing exercises you like and you will stick with it better. Also list your favorite workout resources, videos, books, DVDs etc.

Workout Tracking Pages

Track your workouts. What did you do? How much? How did you feel? See the progress you make day to day!

Rider Fitness Assessment

Date: _____

Fitness Type	Poor	Fair	Good	Great
Flexibility				
Strength				
Cardiovascular				
Balance				
Overall Stability While Riding				

Date: _____

Fitness Type	Poor	Fair	Good	Great
Flexibility				
Strength				
Cardiovascular				
Balance				
Overall Stability While Riding				

Date: _____

Fitness Type	Poor	Fair	Good	Great
Flexibility				
Strength				
Cardiovascular				
Balance				
Overall Stability While Riding				

Date: _____

Fitness Type	Poor	Fair	Good	Great
Flexibility				
Strength				
Cardiovascular				
Balance				
Overall Stability While Riding				

Fitness is for developing your capability by enhancing your ability.

Rider Fitness Goals Worksheet

Riding Skillset Goals	Achieve By	Date Achieved

To reach my goals I plan to:

Workout _____ days a week.

I will be working out at home/gym/outdoors.

Who will you share your progress with for accountability?

_____

I will take _____ riding lessons per month.

What will I tell myself when this gets hard or I don't feel like working out or putting in the training? _____

_____

_____

I hope to feel _____ for sticking with my workouts. When I ride, my workouts will help me to _____

_____

Notes

Exercise to Try	Resource	Like	Don't Like

Favorite Workout Videos, DVDs, or Books

- _____
- _____
- _____
- _____
- _____

Today's Goal _____   (M) (T) (W) (T) (F) (S) (S)

Focus_____ **Date/Time** _____

Stretch ◯   **Warm-Up** _____

Strength/Balance/Flexibility Training

Exercise		Set 1	Set 2	Set 3	Set 4	Set 5
	Reps					
	Weight					
	Reps					
	Weight					
	Reps					
	Weight					
	Reps					
	Weight					
	Reps					
	Weight					
	Reps					
	Weight					
	Reps					
	Weight					
	Reps					
	Weight					
	Reps					
	Weight					
	Reps					
	Weight					

Cardio

Exercise	Calories	Distance	Time

Water Intake _____

Cooldown _____

Feeling ☆ ☆ ☆ ☆ ☆

Notes

Today's Goal _____   (M) (T) (W) (T) (F) (S) (S)

Focus_____ **Date/Time** _____

Stretch ○   **Warm-Up** _____

Strength/Balance/Flexibility Training

Exercise		Set 1	Set 2	Set 3	Set 4	Set 5
	Reps					
	Weight					
	Reps					
	Weight					
	Reps					
	Weight					
	Reps					
	Weight					
	Reps					
	Weight					
	Reps					
	Weight					
	Reps					
	Weight					
	Reps					
	Weight					
	Reps					
	Weight					
	Reps					
	Weight					

Cardio

Exercise	Calories	Distance	Time

Water Intake _____

Cooldown _____

Feeling ☆ ☆ ☆ ☆ ☆

Notes

Today's Goal _____ Ⓜ Ⓣ Ⓦ Ⓣ Ⓕ ● ●

Focus_____ Date/Time _____

Stretch ◯   Warm-Up _____

Strength/Balance/Flexibility Training

Exercise		Set 1	Set 2	Set 3	Set 4	Set 5
	Reps					
	Weight					
	Reps					
	Weight					
	Reps					
	Weight					
	Reps					
	Weight					
	Reps					
	Weight					
	Reps					
	Weight					
	Reps					
	Weight					
	Reps					
	Weight					
	Reps					
	Weight					
	Reps					
	Weight					

Cardio

Exercise	Calories	Distance	Time

Water Intake _____

Cooldown _____

Feeling ☆ ☆ ☆ ☆ ☆

Notes

Today's Goal _____

(M) (T) (W) (T) (F) **(S) (S)**

Focus_____**Date/Time**_____

Stretch ◯   **Warm-Up** _____

Strength/Balance/Flexibility Training

Exercise		Set 1	Set 2	Set 3	Set 4	Set 5
	Reps					
	Weight					
	Reps					
	Weight					
	Reps					
	Weight					
	Reps					
	Weight					
	Reps					
	Weight					
	Reps					
	Weight					
	Reps					
	Weight					
	Reps					
	Weight					
	Reps					
	Weight					
	Reps					
	Weight					

Cardio

Exercise	Calories	Distance	Time

Water Intake _____

Cooldown _____

Feeling ☆ ☆ ☆ ☆ ☆

Notes

Today's Goal _____ Ⓜ Ⓣ Ⓦ Ⓣ Ⓕ ⑤ ⑤

Focus_____ **Date/Time** _____

Stretch ◯   **Warm-Up** _____

Strength/Balance/Flexibility Training

Exercise		Set 1	Set 2	Set 3	Set 4	Set 5
	Reps					
	Weight					
	Reps					
	Weight					
	Reps					
	Weight					
	Reps					
	Weight					
	Reps					
	Weight					
	Reps					
	Weight					
	Reps					
	Weight					
	Reps					
	Weight					
	Reps					
	Weight					
	Reps					
	Weight					

Cardio

Exercise	Calories	Distance	Time

Water Intake _____

Cooldown _____

Feeling ☆ ☆ ☆ ☆ ☆

Notes

Today's Goal _____ Ⓜ Ⓣ Ⓦ Ⓣ Ⓕ ⬤ ⬤

Focus _____ **Date/Time** _____

Stretch ◯   **Warm-Up** _____

Strength/Balance/Flexibility Training

Exercise		Set 1	Set 2	Set 3	Set 4	Set 5
	Reps					
	Weight					
	Reps					
	Weight					
	Reps					
	Weight					
	Reps					
	Weight					
	Reps					
	Weight					
	Reps					
	Weight					
	Reps					
	Weight					
	Reps					
	Weight					
	Reps					
	Weight					
	Reps					
	Weight					

Cardio

Exercise	Calories	Distance	Time

Water Intake _____

Cooldown _____

Feeling ☆ ☆ ☆ ☆ ☆

Notes

Today's Goal _____ Ⓜ Ⓣ Ⓦ Ⓣ Ⓕ ⬤ ⬤

Focus_____**Date/Time**_____

Stretch ◯   **Warm-Up** _____

Strength/Balance/Flexibility Training

Exercise		Set 1	Set 2	Set 3	Set 4	Set 5
	Reps					
	Weight					
	Reps					
	Weight					
	Reps					
	Weight					
	Reps					
	Weight					
	Reps					
	Weight					
	Reps					
	Weight					
	Reps					
	Weight					
	Reps					
	Weight					
	Reps					
	Weight					
	Reps					
	Weight					

Cardio

Exercise	Calories	Distance	Time

Water Intake _____

Cooldown _____

Feeling ☆ ☆ ☆ ☆ ☆

Notes
_____

Today's Goal _____

(M) (T) (W) (T) (F) **(S)** **(S)**

Focus_____ **Date/Time** _____

Stretch ◯   **Warm-Up** _____

Strength/Balance/Flexibility Training

Exercise		Set 1	Set 2	Set 3	Set 4	Set 5
	Reps					
	Weight					
	Reps					
	Weight					
	Reps					
	Weight					
	Reps					
	Weight					
	Reps					
	Weight					
	Reps					
	Weight					
	Reps					
	Weight					
	Reps					
	Weight					
	Reps					
	Weight					
	Reps					
	Weight					

Cardio

Exercise	Calories	Distance	Time

Water Intake _____

Cooldown _____

Feeling ☆ ☆ ☆ ☆ ☆

Notes

_____

Today's Goal _____ Ⓜ Ⓣ Ⓦ Ⓣ Ⓕ ⬤S ⬤S

Focus _____ **Date/Time** _____

Stretch ◯   **Warm-Up** _____

Strength/Balance/Flexibility Training

Exercise		Set 1	Set 2	Set 3	Set 4	Set 5
	Reps					
	Weight					
	Reps					
	Weight					
	Reps					
	Weight					
	Reps					
	Weight					
	Reps					
	Weight					
	Reps					
	Weight					
	Reps					
	Weight					
	Reps					
	Weight					
	Reps					
	Weight					
	Reps					
	Weight					

Cardio

Exercise	Calories	Distance	Time

Water Intake _____

Cooldown _____

Feeling ☆ ☆ ☆ ☆ ☆

Notes

Today's Goal _____ (M) (T) (W) (T) (F) ● ●

Focus_____**Date/Time** _____

Stretch ○   **Warm-Up** _____

Strength/Balance/Flexibility Training

Exercise		Set 1	Set 2	Set 3	Set 4	Set 5
	Reps					
	Weight					
	Reps					
	Weight					
	Reps					
	Weight					
	Reps					
	Weight					
	Reps					
	Weight					
	Reps					
	Weight					
	Reps					
	Weight					
	Reps					
	Weight					
	Reps					
	Weight					
	Reps					
	Weight					

Cardio

Exercise	Calories	Distance	Time

Water Intake _____

Cooldown _____

Feeling ☆ ☆ ☆ ☆ ☆

Notes

Today's Goal _____   (M) (T) (W) (T) (F) (S) (S)

Focus_____**Date/Time** _____

Stretch ◯   **Warm-Up** _____

Strength/Balance/Flexibility Training

Exercise		Set 1	Set 2	Set 3	Set 4	Set 5
	Reps					
	Weight					
	Reps					
	Weight					
	Reps					
	Weight					
	Reps					
	Weight					
	Reps					
	Weight					
	Reps					
	Weight					
	Reps					
	Weight					
	Reps					
	Weight					
	Reps					
	Weight					
	Reps					
	Weight					

Cardio

Exercise	Calories	Distance	Time

Water Intake _____

Cooldown _____

Feeling ☆ ☆ ☆ ☆ ☆

Notes

Today's Goal _____ Ⓜ Ⓣ Ⓦ Ⓣ Ⓕ ● ●

Focus_____**Date/Time** _____

Stretch ◯   **Warm-Up** _____

Strength/Balance/Flexibility Training

Exercise		Set 1	Set 2	Set 3	Set 4	Set 5
	Reps					
	Weight					
	Reps					
	Weight					
	Reps					
	Weight					
	Reps					
	Weight					
	Reps					
	Weight					
	Reps					
	Weight					
	Reps					
	Weight					
	Reps					
	Weight					
	Reps					
	Weight					
	Reps					
	Weight					

Cardio

Exercise	Calories	Distance	Time

Water Intake _____

Cooldown _____

Feeling ☆ ☆ ☆ ☆ ☆

Notes

Today's Goal _____ Ⓜ Ⓣ Ⓦ Ⓣ Ⓕ ⬤ ⬤

Focus_____**Date/Time** _____

Stretch ○   **Warm-Up** _____

Strength/Balance/Flexibility Training

Exercise		Set 1	Set 2	Set 3	Set 4	Set 5
	Reps					
	Weight					
	Reps					
	Weight					
	Reps					
	Weight					
	Reps					
	Weight					
	Reps					
	Weight					
	Reps					
	Weight					
	Reps					
	Weight					
	Reps					
	Weight					
	Reps					
	Weight					
	Reps					
	Weight					

Cardio

Exercise	Calories	Distance	Time

Water Intake _____

Cooldown _____

Feeling ☆ ☆ ☆ ☆ ☆

Notes

Today's Goal _____   Ⓜ Ⓣ Ⓦ Ⓣ Ⓕ 🅢 🅢

Focus_____ Date/Time _____

Stretch ◯   Warm-Up _____

Strength/Balance/Flexibility Training

Exercise		Set 1	Set 2	Set 3	Set 4	Set 5
	Reps					
	Weight					
	Reps					
	Weight					
	Reps					
	Weight					
	Reps					
	Weight					
	Reps					
	Weight					
	Reps					
	Weight					
	Reps					
	Weight					
	Reps					
	Weight					
	Reps					
	Weight					
	Reps					
	Weight					

Cardio

Exercise	Calories	Distance	Time

Water Intake _____

Cooldown _____

Feeling ☆ ☆ ☆ ☆ ☆

Notes

Today's Goal _____ Ⓜ Ⓣ Ⓦ Ⓣ Ⓕ ⚫ ⚫

Focus_____ Date/Time _____

Stretch ◯   **Warm-Up** _____

Strength/Balance/Flexibility Training

Exercise		Set 1	Set 2	Set 3	Set 4	Set 5
	Reps					
	Weight					
	Reps					
	Weight					
	Reps					
	Weight					
	Reps					
	Weight					
	Reps					
	Weight					
	Reps					
	Weight					
	Reps					
	Weight					
	Reps					
	Weight					
	Reps					
	Weight					
	Reps					
	Weight					
	Reps					
	Weight					

Cardio

Exercise	Calories	Distance	Time

Water Intake _____

Cooldown _____

Feeling ☆ ☆ ☆ ☆ ☆

Notes

Today's Goal _____

(M) (T) (W) (T) (F) **(S)** **(S)**

Focus _____ **Date/Time** _____

Stretch ◯   **Warm-Up** _____

Strength/Balance/Flexibility Training

Exercise		Set 1	Set 2	Set 3	Set 4	Set 5
	Reps					
	Weight					
	Reps					
	Weight					
	Reps					
	Weight					
	Reps					
	Weight					
	Reps					
	Weight					
	Reps					
	Weight					
	Reps					
	Weight					
	Reps					
	Weight					
	Reps					
	Weight					
	Reps					
	Weight					

Cardio

Exercise	Calories	Distance	Time

Water Intake _____

Cooldown _____

Feeling ☆ ☆ ☆ ☆ ☆

Notes

Today's Goal _____   (M) (T) (W) (T) (F) (S) (S)

Focus_____ Date/Time _____

Stretch ◯   Warm-Up _____

Strength/Balance/Flexibility Training

Exercise		Set 1	Set 2	Set 3	Set 4	Set 5
	Reps					
	Weight					
	Reps					
	Weight					
	Reps					
	Weight					
	Reps					
	Weight					
	Reps					
	Weight					
	Reps					
	Weight					
	Reps					
	Weight					
	Reps					
	Weight					
	Reps					
	Weight					
	Reps					
	Weight					

Cardio

Exercise	Calories	Distance	Time

Water Intake _____

Cooldown _____

Feeling ☆ ☆ ☆ ☆ ☆

Notes

Today's Goal _____ Ⓜ Ⓣ Ⓦ Ⓣ Ⓕ **Ⓢ Ⓢ**

Focus_____**Date/Time** _____

Stretch ○   **Warm-Up** _____

Strength/Balance/Flexibility Training

Exercise		Set 1	Set 2	Set 3	Set 4	Set 5
	Reps					
	Weight					
	Reps					
	Weight					
	Reps					
	Weight					
	Reps					
	Weight					
	Reps					
	Weight					
	Reps					
	Weight					
	Reps					
	Weight					
	Reps					
	Weight					
	Reps					
	Weight					
	Reps					
	Weight					

Cardio

Exercise	Calories	Distance	Time

Water Intake _____

Cooldown _____

Feeling ☆ ☆ ☆ ☆ ☆

Notes

Today's Goal _____ Ⓜ Ⓣ Ⓦ Ⓣ Ⓕ Ⓢ Ⓢ

Focus_____ **Date/Time** _____

Stretch ◯   **Warm-Up** _____

Strength/Balance/Flexibility Training

Exercise		Set 1	Set 2	Set 3	Set 4	Set 5
	Reps					
	Weight					
	Reps					
	Weight					
	Reps					
	Weight					
	Reps					
	Weight					
	Reps					
	Weight					
	Reps					
	Weight					
	Reps					
	Weight					
	Reps					
	Weight					
	Reps					
	Weight					
	Reps					
	Weight					

Cardio

Exercise	Calories	Distance	Time

Water Intake _____

Cooldown _____

Feeling ☆ ☆ ☆ ☆ ☆

Notes

Today's Goal _____   Ⓜ Ⓣ Ⓦ Ⓣ Ⓕ ⬤ ⬤

Focus_____**Date/Time** _____

Stretch ◯   **Warm-Up** _____

Strength/Balance/Flexibility Training

Exercise		Set 1	Set 2	Set 3	Set 4	Set 5
	Reps					
	Weight					
	Reps					
	Weight					
	Reps					
	Weight					
	Reps					
	Weight					
	Reps					
	Weight					
	Reps					
	Weight					
	Reps					
	Weight					
	Reps					
	Weight					
	Reps					
	Weight					
	Reps					
	Weight					

Cardio

Exercise	Calories	Distance	Time

Water Intake _____

Cooldown _____

Feeling ☆ ☆ ☆ ☆ ☆

Notes

Today's Goal _____ (M) (T) (W) (T) (F) (S) (S)

Focus_____ Date/Time _____

Stretch ○   Warm-Up _____

Strength/Balance/Flexibility Training

Exercise		Set 1	Set 2	Set 3	Set 4	Set 5
	Reps					
	Weight					
	Reps					
	Weight					
	Reps					
	Weight					
	Reps					
	Weight					
	Reps					
	Weight					
	Reps					
	Weight					
	Reps					
	Weight					
	Reps					
	Weight					
	Reps					
	Weight					
	Reps					
	Weight					

Cardio

Exercise	Calories	Distance	Time

Water Intake _____

Cooldown _____

Feeling ☆ ☆ ☆ ☆ ☆

Notes

Today's Goal _____   Ⓜ Ⓣ Ⓦ Ⓣ Ⓕ ⬤ ⬤

Focus_____**Date/Time** _____

Stretch ◯   **Warm-Up** _____

Strength/Balance/Flexibility Training

Exercise		Set 1	Set 2	Set 3	Set 4	Set 5
	Reps					
	Weight					
	Reps					
	Weight					
	Reps					
	Weight					
	Reps					
	Weight					
	Reps					
	Weight					
	Reps					
	Weight					
	Reps					
	Weight					
	Reps					
	Weight					
	Reps					
	Weight					
	Reps					
	Weight					

Cardio

Exercise	Calories	Distance	Time

Water Intake _____

Cooldown _____

Feeling ☆ ☆ ☆ ☆ ☆

Notes

Today's Goal _____

(M) (T) (W) (T) (F) **(S)** **(S)**

Focus _____ **Date/Time** _____

Stretch ○   **Warm-Up** _____

Strength/Balance/Flexibility Training

Exercise		Set 1	Set 2	Set 3	Set 4	Set 5
	Reps					
	Weight					
	Reps					
	Weight					
	Reps					
	Weight					
	Reps					
	Weight					
	Reps					
	Weight					
	Reps					
	Weight					
	Reps					
	Weight					
	Reps					
	Weight					
	Reps					
	Weight					
	Reps					
	Weight					

Cardio

Exercise	Calories	Distance	Time

Water Intake _____

Cooldown _____

Feeling ☆ ☆ ☆ ☆ ☆

Notes

Today's Goal _____ Ⓜ Ⓣ Ⓦ Ⓣ Ⓕ ⬤ ⬤

Focus_____**Date/Time** _____

Stretch ◯   **Warm-Up** _____

Strength/Balance/Flexibility Training

Exercise		Set 1	Set 2	Set 3	Set 4	Set 5
	Reps					
	Weight					
	Reps					
	Weight					
	Reps					
	Weight					
	Reps					
	Weight					
	Reps					
	Weight					
	Reps					
	Weight					
	Reps					
	Weight					
	Reps					
	Weight					
	Reps					
	Weight					
	Reps					
	Weight					

Cardio

Exercise	Calories	Distance	Time

Water Intake _____

Cooldown _____

Feeling ☆ ☆ ☆ ☆ ☆

Notes

Today's Goal _____ (M) (T) (W) (T) (F) **S** **S**

Focus_____ **Date/Time** _____

Stretch ◯   **Warm-Up** _____

Strength/Balance/Flexibility Training

Exercise		Set 1	Set 2	Set 3	Set 4	Set 5
	Reps					
	Weight					
	Reps					
	Weight					
	Reps					
	Weight					
	Reps					
	Weight					
	Reps					
	Weight					
	Reps					
	Weight					
	Reps					
	Weight					
	Reps					
	Weight					
	Reps					
	Weight					
	Reps					
	Weight					

Cardio

Exercise	Calories	Distance	Time

Water Intake _____

Cooldown _____

Feeling ☆ ☆ ☆ ☆ ☆

Notes

Today's Goal _____ Ⓜ Ⓣ Ⓦ Ⓣ Ⓕ 🅢 🅢

Focus _____ Date/Time _____

Stretch ○   Warm-Up _____

Strength/Balance/Flexibility Training

Exercise		Set 1	Set 2	Set 3	Set 4	Set 5
	Reps					
	Weight					
	Reps					
	Weight					
	Reps					
	Weight					
	Reps					
	Weight					
	Reps					
	Weight					
	Reps					
	Weight					
	Reps					
	Weight					
	Reps					
	Weight					
	Reps					
	Weight					
	Reps					
	Weight					

Cardio

Exercise	Calories	Distance	Time

Water Intake _____

Cooldown _____

Feeling ☆ ☆ ☆ ☆ ☆

Notes

Today's Goal _____

(M) (T) (W) (T) (F) (S) (S)

Focus_____ **Date/Time** _____

Stretch ○   **Warm-Up** _____

Strength/Balance/Flexibility Training

Exercise		Set 1	Set 2	Set 3	Set 4	Set 5
	Reps					
	Weight					
	Reps					
	Weight					
	Reps					
	Weight					
	Reps					
	Weight					
	Reps					
	Weight					
	Reps					
	Weight					
	Reps					
	Weight					
	Reps					
	Weight					
	Reps					
	Weight					
	Reps					
	Weight					

Cardio

Exercise	Calories	Distance	Time

Water Intake _____

Cooldown _____

Feeling ☆ ☆ ☆ ☆ ☆

Notes

Today's Goal _____ Ⓜ Ⓣ Ⓦ Ⓣ Ⓕ ⬤ ⬤

Focus_____**Date/Time** _____

Stretch ◯   **Warm-Up** _____

Strength/Balance/Flexibility Training

Exercise		Set 1	Set 2	Set 3	Set 4	Set 5
	Reps					
	Weight					
	Reps					
	Weight					
	Reps					
	Weight					
	Reps					
	Weight					
	Reps					
	Weight					
	Reps					
	Weight					
	Reps					
	Weight					
	Reps					
	Weight					
	Reps					
	Weight					
	Reps					
	Weight					

Cardio

Exercise	Calories	Distance	Time

Water Intake _____

Cooldown _____

Feeling ☆ ☆ ☆ ☆ ☆

Notes

Today's Goal _____ Ⓜ Ⓣ Ⓦ Ⓣ Ⓕ 🅢 🅢

Focus_____ **Date/Time** _____

Stretch ◯   **Warm-Up** _____

Strength/Balance/Flexibility Training

Exercise		Set 1	Set 2	Set 3	Set 4	Set 5
	Reps					
	Weight					
	Reps					
	Weight					
	Reps					
	Weight					
	Reps					
	Weight					
	Reps					
	Weight					
	Reps					
	Weight					
	Reps					
	Weight					
	Reps					
	Weight					
	Reps					
	Weight					
	Reps					
	Weight					

Cardio

Exercise	Calories	Distance	Time

Water Intake _____

Cooldown _____

Feeling ☆ ☆ ☆ ☆ ☆

Notes

Today's Goal _____ Ⓜ Ⓣ Ⓦ Ⓣ Ⓕ ⑤ ⑤

Focus_____**Date/Time** _____

Stretch ◯   **Warm-Up** _____

Strength/Balance/Flexibility Training

Exercise		Set 1	Set 2	Set 3	Set 4	Set 5
	Reps					
	Weight					
	Reps					
	Weight					
	Reps					
	Weight					
	Reps					
	Weight					
	Reps					
	Weight					
	Reps					
	Weight					
	Reps					
	Weight					
	Reps					
	Weight					
	Reps					
	Weight					
	Reps					
	Weight					

Cardio

Exercise	Calories	Distance	Time

Water Intake _____

Cooldown _____

Feeling ☆ ☆ ☆ ☆ ☆

Notes

Today's Goal

_____ Ⓜ Ⓣ Ⓦ Ⓣ Ⓕ Ⓢ Ⓢ

Focus_____**Date/Time** _____

Stretch ◯   **Warm-Up** _____

Strength/Balance/Flexibility Training

Exercise		Set 1	Set 2	Set 3	Set 4	Set 5
	Reps					
	Weight					
	Reps					
	Weight					
	Reps					
	Weight					
	Reps					
	Weight					
	Reps					
	Weight					
	Reps					
	Weight					
	Reps					
	Weight					
	Reps					
	Weight					
	Reps					
	Weight					
	Reps					
	Weight					

Cardio

Exercise	Calories	Distance	Time

Water Intake _____

Cooldown _____

Feeling ☆ ☆ ☆ ☆ ☆

Notes

Today's Goal _____ Ⓜ Ⓣ Ⓦ Ⓣ Ⓕ ● ●

Focus_____**Date/Time** _____

Stretch ◯   **Warm-Up** _____

Strength/Balance/Flexibility Training

Exercise		Set 1	Set 2	Set 3	Set 4	Set 5
	Reps					
	Weight					
	Reps					
	Weight					
	Reps					
	Weight					
	Reps					
	Weight					
	Reps					
	Weight					
	Reps					
	Weight					
	Reps					
	Weight					
	Reps					
	Weight					
	Reps					
	Weight					
	Reps					
	Weight					

Cardio

Exercise	Calories	Distance	Time

Water Intake _____

Cooldown _____

Feeling ☆ ☆ ☆ ☆ ☆

Notes

Today's Goal _____ Ⓜ Ⓣ Ⓦ Ⓣ Ⓕ ⬤ ⬤

Focus_____**Date/Time** _____

Stretch ◯　　　**Warm-Up** _____

Strength/Balance/Flexibility Training

Exercise		Set 1	Set 2	Set 3	Set 4	Set 5
	Reps					
	Weight					
	Reps					
	Weight					
	Reps					
	Weight					
	Reps					
	Weight					
	Reps					
	Weight					
	Reps					
	Weight					
	Reps					
	Weight					
	Reps					
	Weight					
	Reps					
	Weight					
	Reps					
	Weight					

Cardio

Exercise	Calories	Distance	Time

Water Intake _____

Cooldown _____

Feeling ☆ ☆ ☆ ☆ ☆

Notes

Today's Goal _____

(M) (T) (W) (T) (F) ● ●

Focus_____**Date/Time**_____

Stretch ○   **Warm-Up** _____

Strength/Balance/Flexibility Training

Exercise		Set 1	Set 2	Set 3	Set 4	Set 5
	Reps					
	Weight					
	Reps					
	Weight					
	Reps					
	Weight					
	Reps					
	Weight					
	Reps					
	Weight					
	Reps					
	Weight					
	Reps					
	Weight					
	Reps					
	Weight					
	Reps					
	Weight					
	Reps					
	Weight					

Cardio

Exercise	Calories	Distance	Time

Water Intake _____

Cooldown _____

Feeling ☆ ☆ ☆ ☆ ☆

Notes

Today's Goal _____ Ⓜ Ⓣ Ⓦ Ⓣ Ⓕ ⬤S ⬤S

Focus _____ **Date/Time** _____

Stretch ◯   **Warm-Up** _____

Strength/Balance/Flexibility Training

Exercise		Set 1	Set 2	Set 3	Set 4	Set 5
	Reps					
	Weight					
	Reps					
	Weight					
	Reps					
	Weight					
	Reps					
	Weight					
	Reps					
	Weight					
	Reps					
	Weight					
	Reps					
	Weight					
	Reps					
	Weight					
	Reps					
	Weight					
	Reps					
	Weight					

Cardio

Exercise	Calories	Distance	Time

Water Intake _____

Cooldown _____

Feeling ☆ ☆ ☆ ☆ ☆

Notes
_____
_____

Today's Goal _____   (M) (T) (W) (T) (F) ⬤ ⬤

Focus_____**Date/Time** _____

Stretch ◯   **Warm-Up** _____

Strength/Balance/Flexibility Training

Exercise		Set 1	Set 2	Set 3	Set 4	Set 5
	Reps					
	Weight					
	Reps					
	Weight					
	Reps					
	Weight					
	Reps					
	Weight					
	Reps					
	Weight					
	Reps					
	Weight					
	Reps					
	Weight					
	Reps					
	Weight					
	Reps					
	Weight					
	Reps					
	Weight					

Cardio

Exercise	Calories	Distance	Time

Water Intake _____

Cooldown _____

Feeling ☆ ☆ ☆ ☆ ☆

Notes

Today's Goal _____ (M)(T)(W)(T)(F)(S)(S)

Focus_____ Date/Time _____

Stretch ○   Warm-Up _____

Strength/Balance/Flexibility Training

Exercise		Set 1	Set 2	Set 3	Set 4	Set 5
	Reps					
	Weight					
	Reps					
	Weight					
	Reps					
	Weight					
	Reps					
	Weight					
	Reps					
	Weight					
	Reps					
	Weight					
	Reps					
	Weight					
	Reps					
	Weight					
	Reps					
	Weight					
	Reps					
	Weight					

Cardio

Exercise	Calories	Distance	Time

Water Intake _____

Cooldown _____

Feeling ☆ ☆ ☆ ☆ ☆

Notes

Today's Goal _____ Ⓜ Ⓣ Ⓦ Ⓣ Ⓕ 🅢 🅢

Focus_____**Date/Time** _____

Stretch ◯   **Warm-Up** _____

Strength/Balance/Flexibility Training

Exercise		Set 1	Set 2	Set 3	Set 4	Set 5
	Reps					
	Weight					
	Reps					
	Weight					
	Reps					
	Weight					
	Reps					
	Weight					
	Reps					
	Weight					
	Reps					
	Weight					
	Reps					
	Weight					
	Reps					
	Weight					
	Reps					
	Weight					
	Reps					
	Weight					

Cardio

Exercise	Calories	Distance	Time

Water Intake _____

Cooldown _____

Feeling ☆ ☆ ☆ ☆ ☆

Notes

Today's Goal _____ (M) (T) (W) (T) (F) **(S)** **(S)**

Focus _____ **Date/Time** _____

Stretch ◯   **Warm-Up** _____

Strength/Balance/Flexibility Training

Exercise		Set 1	Set 2	Set 3	Set 4	Set 5
	Reps					
	Weight					
	Reps					
	Weight					
	Reps					
	Weight					
	Reps					
	Weight					
	Reps					
	Weight					
	Reps					
	Weight					
	Reps					
	Weight					
	Reps					
	Weight					
	Reps					
	Weight					
	Reps					
	Weight					

Cardio

Exercise	Calories	Distance	Time

Water Intake _____

Cooldown _____

Feeling ☆ ☆ ☆ ☆ ☆

Notes

Today's Goal _____   (M) (T) (W) (T) (F) **S** **S**

Focus_____Date/Time _____

Stretch ◯   Warm-Up _____

Strength/Balance/Flexibility Training

Exercise		Set 1	Set 2	Set 3	Set 4	Set 5
	Reps					
	Weight					
	Reps					
	Weight					
	Reps					
	Weight					
	Reps					
	Weight					
	Reps					
	Weight					
	Reps					
	Weight					
	Reps					
	Weight					
	Reps					
	Weight					
	Reps					
	Weight					
	Reps					
	Weight					

Cardio

Exercise	Calories	Distance	Time

Water Intake _____

Cooldown _____

Feeling ☆ ☆ ☆ ☆ ☆

Notes

Today's Goal _____ Ⓜ Ⓣ Ⓦ Ⓣ Ⓕ 🅢 🅢

Focus_____**Date/Time** _____

Stretch ◯   **Warm-Up** _____

Strength/Balance/Flexibility Training

Exercise		Set 1	Set 2	Set 3	Set 4	Set 5
	Reps					
	Weight					
	Reps					
	Weight					
	Reps					
	Weight					
	Reps					
	Weight					
	Reps					
	Weight					
	Reps					
	Weight					
	Reps					
	Weight					
	Reps					
	Weight					
	Reps					
	Weight					
	Reps					
	Weight					

Cardio

Exercise	Calories	Distance	Time

Water Intake _____

Cooldown _____

Feeling ☆ ☆ ☆ ☆ ☆

Notes

Today's Goal _____   Ⓜ Ⓣ Ⓦ Ⓣ Ⓕ ⬤ ⬤

Focus_____ **Date/Time** _____

Stretch ◯   **Warm-Up** _____

Strength/Balance/Flexibility Training

Exercise		Set 1	Set 2	Set 3	Set 4	Set 5
	Reps					
	Weight					
	Reps					
	Weight					
	Reps					
	Weight					
	Reps					
	Weight					
	Reps					
	Weight					
	Reps					
	Weight					
	Reps					
	Weight					
	Reps					
	Weight					
	Reps					
	Weight					
	Reps					
	Weight					

Cardio

Exercise	Calories	Distance	Time

Water Intake _____

Cooldown _____

Feeling ☆ ☆ ☆ ☆ ☆

Notes

_____

Today's Goal _____ (M) (T) (W) (T) (F) (S) (S)

Focus_____**Date/Time** _____

Stretch ◯   **Warm-Up** _____

Strength/Balance/Flexibility Training

Exercise		Set 1	Set 2	Set 3	Set 4	Set 5
	Reps					
	Weight					
	Reps					
	Weight					
	Reps					
	Weight					
	Reps					
	Weight					
	Reps					
	Weight					
	Reps					
	Weight					
	Reps					
	Weight					
	Reps					
	Weight					
	Reps					
	Weight					
	Reps					
	Weight					

Cardio

Exercise	Calories	Distance	Time

Water Intake _____

Cooldown _____

Feeling ☆ ☆ ☆ ☆ ☆

Notes
_____

Today's Goal _____

Focus_____**Date/Time** _____

Stretch ○   **Warm-Up** _____

Strength/Balance/Flexibility Training

Exercise		Set 1	Set 2	Set 3	Set 4	Set 5
	Reps					
	Weight					
	Reps					
	Weight					
	Reps					
	Weight					
	Reps					
	Weight					
	Reps					
	Weight					
	Reps					
	Weight					
	Reps					
	Weight					
	Reps					
	Weight					
	Reps					
	Weight					
	Reps					
	Weight					

Cardio

Exercise	Calories	Distance	Time

Water Intake _____

Cooldown _____

Feeling ☆ ☆ ☆ ☆ ☆

Notes

Today's Goal _____ Ⓜ Ⓣ Ⓦ Ⓣ Ⓕ ⬤ ⬤

Focus_____**Date/Time** _____

Stretch ◯ **Warm-Up** _____

Strength/Balance/Flexibility Training

Exercise		Set 1	Set 2	Set 3	Set 4	Set 5
	Reps					
	Weight					
	Reps					
	Weight					
	Reps					
	Weight					
	Reps					
	Weight					
	Reps					
	Weight					
	Reps					
	Weight					
	Reps					
	Weight					
	Reps					
	Weight					
	Reps					
	Weight					
	Reps					
	Weight					

Cardio

Exercise	Calories	Distance	Time

Water Intake _____

Cooldown _____

Feeling ☆ ☆ ☆ ☆ ☆

Notes

Today's Goal _____ Ⓜ Ⓣ Ⓦ Ⓣ Ⓕ 🅢 🅢

Focus_____**Date/Time** _____

Stretch ◯   **Warm-Up** _____

Strength/Balance/Flexibility Training

Exercise		Set 1	Set 2	Set 3	Set 4	Set 5
	Reps					
	Weight					
	Reps					
	Weight					
	Reps					
	Weight					
	Reps					
	Weight					
	Reps					
	Weight					
	Reps					
	Weight					
	Reps					
	Weight					
	Reps					
	Weight					
	Reps					
	Weight					
	Reps					
	Weight					

Cardio

Exercise	Calories	Distance	Time

Water Intake _____

Cooldown _____

Feeling ☆ ☆ ☆ ☆ ☆

Notes

Today's Goal _____   Ⓜ Ⓣ Ⓦ Ⓣ Ⓕ Ⓢ Ⓢ

Focus_____**Date/Time** _____

Stretch ◯   **Warm-Up** _____

Strength/Balance/Flexibility Training

Exercise		Set 1	Set 2	Set 3	Set 4	Set 5
	Reps					
	Weight					
	Reps					
	Weight					
	Reps					
	Weight					
	Reps					
	Weight					
	Reps					
	Weight					
	Reps					
	Weight					
	Reps					
	Weight					
	Reps					
	Weight					
	Reps					
	Weight					
	Reps					
	Weight					

Cardio

Exercise	Calories	Distance	Time

Water Intake _____

Cooldown _____

Feeling ☆ ☆ ☆ ☆ ☆

Notes

Today's Goal _____ Ⓜ Ⓣ Ⓦ Ⓣ Ⓕ 🅢 🅢

Focus_____**Date/Time** _____

Stretch ◯   **Warm-Up** _____

Strength/Balance/Flexibility Training

Exercise		Set 1	Set 2	Set 3	Set 4	Set 5
	Reps					
	Weight					
	Reps					
	Weight					
	Reps					
	Weight					
	Reps					
	Weight					
	Reps					
	Weight					
	Reps					
	Weight					
	Reps					
	Weight					
	Reps					
	Weight					
	Reps					
	Weight					
	Reps					
	Weight					

Cardio

Exercise	Calories	Distance	Time

Water Intake _____

Cooldown _____

Feeling ☆ ☆ ☆ ☆ ☆

Notes

Today's Goal _____   (M) (T) (W) (T) (F) (S) (S)

Focus_____**Date/Time** _____

Stretch ◯   **Warm-Up** _____

Strength/Balance/Flexibility Training

Exercise		Set 1	Set 2	Set 3	Set 4	Set 5
	Reps					
	Weight					
	Reps					
	Weight					
	Reps					
	Weight					
	Reps					
	Weight					
	Reps					
	Weight					
	Reps					
	Weight					
	Reps					
	Weight					
	Reps					
	Weight					
	Reps					
	Weight					
	Reps					
	Weight					

Cardio

Exercise	Calories	Distance	Time

Water Intake _____

Cooldown _____

Feeling ☆ ☆ ☆ ☆ ☆

Notes

Today's Goal _____   Ⓜ Ⓣ Ⓦ Ⓣ Ⓕ ⬤ ⬤

Focus_____**Date/Time** _____

Stretch ◯   **Warm-Up** _____

Strength/Balance/Flexibility Training

Exercise		Set 1	Set 2	Set 3	Set 4	Set 5
	Reps					
	Weight					
	Reps					
	Weight					
	Reps					
	Weight					
	Reps					
	Weight					
	Reps					
	Weight					
	Reps					
	Weight					
	Reps					
	Weight					
	Reps					
	Weight					
	Reps					
	Weight					
	Reps					
	Weight					

Cardio

Exercise	Calories	Distance	Time

Water Intake _____

Cooldown _____

Feeling ☆ ☆ ☆ ☆ ☆

Notes

Today's Goal _____ Ⓜ Ⓣ Ⓦ Ⓣ Ⓕ ⬤ ⬤

Focus_____ **Date/Time** _____

Stretch ◯   **Warm-Up** _____

Strength/Balance/Flexibility Training

Exercise		Set 1	Set 2	Set 3	Set 4	Set 5
	Reps					
	Weight					
	Reps					
	Weight					
	Reps					
	Weight					
	Reps					
	Weight					
	Reps					
	Weight					
	Reps					
	Weight					
	Reps					
	Weight					
	Reps					
	Weight					
	Reps					
	Weight					
	Reps					
	Weight					

Cardio

Exercise	Calories	Distance	Time

Water Intake _____

Cooldown _____

Feeling ☆ ☆ ☆ ☆ ☆

Notes

Today's Goal _____ Ⓜ Ⓣ Ⓦ Ⓣ Ⓕ 🅢 🅢

Focus_____**Date/Time** _____

Stretch ○   **Warm-Up** _____

Strength/Balance/Flexibility Training

Exercise		Set 1	Set 2	Set 3	Set 4	Set 5
	Reps					
	Weight					
	Reps					
	Weight					
	Reps					
	Weight					
	Reps					
	Weight					
	Reps					
	Weight					
	Reps					
	Weight					
	Reps					
	Weight					
	Reps					
	Weight					
	Reps					
	Weight					
	Reps					
	Weight					

Cardio

Exercise	Calories	Distance	Time

Water Intake _____

Cooldown _____

Feeling ☆ ☆ ☆ ☆ ☆

Notes

Today's Goal _____ Ⓜ Ⓣ Ⓦ Ⓣ Ⓕ ⬤ ⬤

Focus_____ **Date/Time** _____

Stretch ◯　　**Warm-Up** _____

Strength/Balance/Flexibility Training

Exercise		Set 1	Set 2	Set 3	Set 4	Set 5
	Reps					
	Weight					
	Reps					
	Weight					
	Reps					
	Weight					
	Reps					
	Weight					
	Reps					
	Weight					
	Reps					
	Weight					
	Reps					
	Weight					
	Reps					
	Weight					
	Reps					
	Weight					
	Reps					
	Weight					

Cardio

Exercise	Calories	Distance	Time

Water Intake _____

Cooldown _____

Feeling ☆ ☆ ☆ ☆ ☆

Notes

Today's Goal _____

(M) (T) (W) (T) (F) **S** **S**

Focus_____ Date/Time _____

Stretch ○   Warm-Up _____

Strength/Balance/Flexibility Training

Exercise		Set 1	Set 2	Set 3	Set 4	Set 5
	Reps					
	Weight					
	Reps					
	Weight					
	Reps					
	Weight					
	Reps					
	Weight					
	Reps					
	Weight					
	Reps					
	Weight					
	Reps					
	Weight					
	Reps					
	Weight					
	Reps					
	Weight					
	Reps					
	Weight					

Cardio

Exercise	Calories	Distance	Time

Water Intake _____

Cooldown _____

Feeling ☆ ☆ ☆ ☆ ☆

Notes

Today's Goal _____ (M) (T) (W) (T) (F) (S) (S)

Focus_____ **Date/Time** _____

Stretch ◯   **Warm-Up** _____

Strength/Balance/Flexibility Training

Exercise		Set 1	Set 2	Set 3	Set 4	Set 5
	Reps					
	Weight					
	Reps					
	Weight					
	Reps					
	Weight					
	Reps					
	Weight					
	Reps					
	Weight					
	Reps					
	Weight					
	Reps					
	Weight					
	Reps					
	Weight					
	Reps					
	Weight					
	Reps					
	Weight					

Cardio

Exercise	Calories	Distance	Time

Water Intake _____

Cooldown _____

Feeling ☆ ☆ ☆ ☆ ☆

Notes

Today's Goal _____ Ⓜ Ⓣ Ⓦ Ⓣ Ⓕ ⬤ ⬤

Focus_____Date/Time _____

Stretch ◯   Warm-Up _____

Strength/Balance/Flexibility Training

Exercise		Set 1	Set 2	Set 3	Set 4	Set 5
	Reps					
	Weight					
	Reps					
	Weight					
	Reps					
	Weight					
	Reps					
	Weight					
	Reps					
	Weight					
	Reps					
	Weight					
	Reps					
	Weight					
	Reps					
	Weight					
	Reps					
	Weight					
	Reps					
	Weight					

Cardio

Exercise	Calories	Distance	Time

Water Intake _____

Cooldown _____

Feeling ☆ ☆ ☆ ☆ ☆

Notes

Today's Goal _____

(M) (T) (W) (T) (F) **(S)** **(S)**

Focus_____ **Date/Time** _____

Stretch ◯   **Warm-Up** _____

Strength/Balance/Flexibility Training

Exercise		Set 1	Set 2	Set 3	Set 4	Set 5
	Reps					
	Weight					
	Reps					
	Weight					
	Reps					
	Weight					
	Reps					
	Weight					
	Reps					
	Weight					
	Reps					
	Weight					
	Reps					
	Weight					
	Reps					
	Weight					
	Reps					
	Weight					
	Reps					
	Weight					

Cardio

Exercise	Calories	Distance	Time

Water Intake _____

Cooldown _____

Feeling ☆ ☆ ☆ ☆ ☆

Notes

_____

Today's Goal _____ (M) (T) (W) (T) (F) **(S)** **(S)**

Focus _____ **Date/Time** _____

Stretch ◯   **Warm-Up** _____

Strength/Balance/Flexibility Training

Exercise		Set 1	Set 2	Set 3	Set 4	Set 5
	Reps					
	Weight					
	Reps					
	Weight					
	Reps					
	Weight					
	Reps					
	Weight					
	Reps					
	Weight					
	Reps					
	Weight					
	Reps					
	Weight					
	Reps					
	Weight					
	Reps					
	Weight					
	Reps					
	Weight					

Cardio

Exercise	Calories	Distance	Time

Water Intake _____

Cooldown _____

Feeling ☆ ☆ ☆ ☆ ☆

Notes

Today's Goal _____ Ⓜ Ⓣ Ⓦ Ⓣ Ⓕ 🅢 🅢

Focus_____**Date/Time** _____

Stretch ◯   **Warm-Up** _____

Strength/Balance/Flexibility Training

Exercise		Set 1	Set 2	Set 3	Set 4	Set 5
	Reps					
	Weight					
	Reps					
	Weight					
	Reps					
	Weight					
	Reps					
	Weight					
	Reps					
	Weight					
	Reps					
	Weight					
	Reps					
	Weight					
	Reps					
	Weight					
	Reps					
	Weight					
	Reps					
	Weight					

Cardio

Exercise	Calories	Distance	Time

Water Intake _____

Cooldown _____

Feeling ☆ ☆ ☆ ☆ ☆

Notes

Today's Goal _____   (M) (T) (W) (T) (F) (S) (S)

Focus_____**Date/Time** _____

Stretch ◯   **Warm-Up** _____

Strength/Balance/Flexibility Training

Exercise		Set 1	Set 2	Set 3	Set 4	Set 5
	Reps					
	Weight					
	Reps					
	Weight					
	Reps					
	Weight					
	Reps					
	Weight					
	Reps					
	Weight					
	Reps					
	Weight					
	Reps					
	Weight					
	Reps					
	Weight					
	Reps					
	Weight					
	Reps					
	Weight					

Cardio

Exercise	Calories	Distance	Time

Water Intake _____

Cooldown _____

Feeling ☆ ☆ ☆ ☆ ☆

Notes

Today's Goal _____   (M) (T) (W) (T) (F) (S) (S)

Focus_____**Date/Time** _____

Stretch ◯   **Warm-Up** _____

Strength/Balance/Flexibility Training

Exercise		Set 1	Set 2	Set 3	Set 4	Set 5
	Reps					
	Weight					
	Reps					
	Weight					
	Reps					
	Weight					
	Reps					
	Weight					
	Reps					
	Weight					
	Reps					
	Weight					
	Reps					
	Weight					
	Reps					
	Weight					
	Reps					
	Weight					
	Reps					
	Weight					

Cardio

Exercise	Calories	Distance	Time

Water Intake _____

Cooldown _____

Feeling ☆ ☆ ☆ ☆ ☆

Notes

Today's Goal _____ Ⓜ Ⓣ Ⓦ Ⓣ Ⓕ 🅢 🅢

Focus_____ **Date/Time** _____

Stretch ◯   **Warm-Up** _____

Strength/Balance/Flexibility Training

Exercise		Set 1	Set 2	Set 3	Set 4	Set 5
	Reps					
	Weight					
	Reps					
	Weight					
	Reps					
	Weight					
	Reps					
	Weight					
	Reps					
	Weight					
	Reps					
	Weight					
	Reps					
	Weight					
	Reps					
	Weight					
	Reps					
	Weight					
	Reps					
	Weight					

Cardio

Exercise	Calories	Distance	Time

Water Intake _____

Cooldown _____

Feeling ☆ ☆ ☆ ☆ ☆

Notes

Today's Goal _____ Ⓜ Ⓣ Ⓦ Ⓣ Ⓕ ⚫S ⚫S

Focus_____ **Date/Time** _____

Stretch ◯   **Warm-Up** _____

Strength/Balance/Flexibility Training

Exercise		Set 1	Set 2	Set 3	Set 4	Set 5
	Reps					
	Weight					
	Reps					
	Weight					
	Reps					
	Weight					
	Reps					
	Weight					
	Reps					
	Weight					
	Reps					
	Weight					
	Reps					
	Weight					
	Reps					
	Weight					
	Reps					
	Weight					
	Reps					
	Weight					

Cardio

Exercise	Calories	Distance	Time

Water Intake _____

Cooldown _____

Feeling ☆ ☆ ☆ ☆ ☆

Notes

Today's Goal _____ Ⓜ Ⓣ Ⓦ Ⓣ Ⓕ ⬤ ⬤

Focus_____**Date/Time** _____

Stretch ◯   **Warm-Up** _____

Strength/Balance/Flexibility Training

Exercise		Set 1	Set 2	Set 3	Set 4	Set 5
	Reps					
	Weight					
	Reps					
	Weight					
	Reps					
	Weight					
	Reps					
	Weight					
	Reps					
	Weight					
	Reps					
	Weight					
	Reps					
	Weight					
	Reps					
	Weight					
	Reps					
	Weight					
	Reps					
	Weight					

Cardio

Exercise	Calories	Distance	Time

Water Intake _____

Cooldown _____

Feeling ☆ ☆ ☆ ☆ ☆

Notes

Today's Goal _____

(M) (T) (W) (T) (F) **(S)** **(S)**

Focus_____ Date/Time _____

Stretch ◯   **Warm-Up** _____

Strength/Balance/Flexibility Training

Exercise		Set 1	Set 2	Set 3	Set 4	Set 5
	Reps					
	Weight					
	Reps					
	Weight					
	Reps					
	Weight					
	Reps					
	Weight					
	Reps					
	Weight					
	Reps					
	Weight					
	Reps					
	Weight					
	Reps					
	Weight					
	Reps					
	Weight					
	Reps					
	Weight					

Cardio

Exercise	Calories	Distance	Time

Water Intake _____

Cooldown _____

Feeling ☆ ☆ ☆ ☆ ☆

Notes

Today's Goal _____ Ⓜ Ⓣ Ⓦ Ⓣ Ⓕ ⬤ ⬤

Focus_____ Date/Time _____

Stretch ◯   Warm-Up _____

Strength/Balance/Flexibility Training

Exercise		Set 1	Set 2	Set 3	Set 4	Set 5
	Reps					
	Weight					
	Reps					
	Weight					
	Reps					
	Weight					
	Reps					
	Weight					
	Reps					
	Weight					
	Reps					
	Weight					
	Reps					
	Weight					
	Reps					
	Weight					
	Reps					
	Weight					
	Reps					
	Weight					

Cardio

Exercise	Calories	Distance	Time

Water Intake _____

Cooldown _____

Feeling ☆ ☆ ☆ ☆ ☆

Notes

Today's Goal _____ Ⓜ Ⓣ Ⓦ Ⓣ Ⓕ ⬤ ⬤

Focus_____**Date/Time**_____

Stretch ◯   **Warm-Up** _____

Strength/Balance/Flexibility Training

Exercise		Set 1	Set 2	Set 3	Set 4	Set 5
	Reps					
	Weight					
	Reps					
	Weight					
	Reps					
	Weight					
	Reps					
	Weight					
	Reps					
	Weight					
	Reps					
	Weight					
	Reps					
	Weight					
	Reps					
	Weight					
	Reps					
	Weight					
	Reps					
	Weight					

Cardio

Exercise	Calories	Distance	Time

Water Intake _____

Cooldown _____

Feeling ☆ ☆ ☆ ☆ ☆

Notes

Today's Goal _____   (M) (T) (W) (T) (F) (S) (S)

Focus_____**Date/Time** _____

Stretch ◯   **Warm-Up** _____

Strength/Balance/Flexibility Training

Exercise		Set 1	Set 2	Set 3	Set 4	Set 5
	Reps					
	Weight					
	Reps					
	Weight					
	Reps					
	Weight					
	Reps					
	Weight					
	Reps					
	Weight					
	Reps					
	Weight					
	Reps					
	Weight					
	Reps					
	Weight					
	Reps					
	Weight					
	Reps					
	Weight					

Cardio

Exercise	Calories	Distance	Time

Water Intake _____

Cooldown _____

Feeling ☆ ☆ ☆ ☆ ☆

Notes

Today's Goal _____ Ⓜ Ⓣ Ⓦ Ⓣ Ⓕ ⬤ ⬤

Focus_____**Date/Time** _____

Stretch ◯   **Warm-Up** _____

Strength/Balance/Flexibility Training

Exercise		Set 1	Set 2	Set 3	Set 4	Set 5
	Reps					
	Weight					
	Reps					
	Weight					
	Reps					
	Weight					
	Reps					
	Weight					
	Reps					
	Weight					
	Reps					
	Weight					
	Reps					
	Weight					
	Reps					
	Weight					
	Reps					
	Weight					
	Reps					
	Weight					

Cardio

Exercise	Calories	Distance	Time

Water Intake _____

Cooldown _____

Feeling ☆ ☆ ☆ ☆ ☆

Notes

Today's Goal _____ Ⓜ Ⓣ Ⓦ Ⓣ Ⓕ ● ●

Focus_____**Date/Time** _____

Stretch ○   **Warm-Up** _____

Strength/Balance/Flexibility Training

Exercise		Set 1	Set 2	Set 3	Set 4	Set 5
	Reps					
	Weight					
	Reps					
	Weight					
	Reps					
	Weight					
	Reps					
	Weight					
	Reps					
	Weight					
	Reps					
	Weight					
	Reps					
	Weight					
	Reps					
	Weight					
	Reps					
	Weight					
	Reps					
	Weight					

Cardio

Exercise	Calories	Distance	Time

Water Intake _____

Cooldown _____

Feeling ☆ ☆ ☆ ☆ ☆

Notes

Today's Goal _____ (M) (T) (W) (T) (F) (S) (S)

Focus _____ Date/Time _____

Stretch ⃝   Warm-Up _____

Strength/Balance/Flexibility Training

Exercise		Set 1	Set 2	Set 3	Set 4	Set 5
	Reps					
	Weight					
	Reps					
	Weight					
	Reps					
	Weight					
	Reps					
	Weight					
	Reps					
	Weight					
	Weight					
	Reps					
	Weight					
	Reps					
	Weight					
	Reps					
	Weight					
	Reps					
	Weight					
	Reps					
	Weight					
	Reps					
	Weight					

Cardio

Exercise	Calories	Distance	Time

Water Intake _____

Cooldown _____

Feeling ☆ ☆ ☆ ☆ ☆

Notes

Today's Goal _____ Ⓜ Ⓣ Ⓦ Ⓣ Ⓕ ⬤S ⬤S

Focus _____ **Date/Time** _____

Stretch ◯   **Warm-Up** _____

Strength/Balance/Flexibility Training

Exercise		Set 1	Set 2	Set 3	Set 4	Set 5
	Reps					
	Weight					
	Reps					
	Weight					
	Reps					
	Weight					
	Reps					
	Weight					
	Reps					
	Weight					
	Reps					
	Weight					
	Reps					
	Weight					
	Reps					
	Weight					
	Reps					
	Weight					
	Reps					
	Weight					

Cardio

Exercise	Calories	Distance	Time

Water Intake _____

Cooldown _____

Feeling ☆ ☆ ☆ ☆ ☆

Notes

Today's Goal _____

(M) (T) (W) (T) (F) **(S) (S)**

Focus_____ **Date/Time** _____

Stretch ◯   **Warm-Up** _____

Strength/Balance/Flexibility Training

Exercise		Set 1	Set 2	Set 3	Set 4	Set 5
	Reps					
	Weight					
	Reps					
	Weight					
	Reps					
	Weight					
	Reps					
	Weight					
	Reps					
	Weight					
	Reps					
	Weight					
	Reps					
	Weight					
	Reps					
	Weight					
	Reps					
	Weight					
	Reps					
	Weight					

Cardio

Exercise	Calories	Distance	Time

Water Intake _____

Cooldown _____

Feeling ☆ ☆ ☆ ☆ ☆

Notes

Today's Goal _____   Ⓜ Ⓣ Ⓦ Ⓣ Ⓕ ⬤S ⬤S

Focus_____**Date/Time** _____

Stretch ◯   **Warm-Up** _____

Strength/Balance/Flexibility Training

Exercise		Set 1	Set 2	Set 3	Set 4	Set 5
	Reps					
	Weight					
	Reps					
	Weight					
	Reps					
	Weight					
	Reps					
	Weight					
	Reps					
	Weight					
	Reps					
	Weight					
	Reps					
	Weight					
	Reps					
	Weight					
	Reps					
	Weight					
	Reps					
	Weight					

Cardio

Exercise	Calories	Distance	Time

Water Intake _____

Cooldown _____

Feeling ☆ ☆ ☆ ☆ ☆

Notes

Today's Goal _____   (M)(T)(W)(T)(F)(S)(S)

Focus_____ **Date/Time** _____

Stretch ○   **Warm-Up** _____

Strength/Balance/Flexibility Training

Exercise		Set 1	Set 2	Set 3	Set 4	Set 5
	Reps					
	Weight					
	Reps					
	Weight					
	Reps					
	Weight					
	Reps					
	Weight					
	Reps					
	Weight					
	Reps					
	Weight					
	Reps					
	Weight					
	Reps					
	Weight					
	Reps					
	Weight					
	Reps					
	Weight					

Cardio

Exercise	Calories	Distance	Time

Water Intake _____

Cooldown _____

Feeling ☆ ☆ ☆ ☆ ☆

Notes

Today's Goal _____ (M) (T) (W) (T) (F) (S) (S)

Focus_____ Date/Time _____

Stretch ○   Warm-Up _____

Strength/Balance/Flexibility Training

Exercise		Set 1	Set 2	Set 3	Set 4	Set 5
	Reps					
	Weight					
	Reps					
	Weight					
	Reps					
	Weight					
	Reps					
	Weight					
	Reps					
	Weight					
	Reps					
	Weight					
	Reps					
	Weight					
	Reps					
	Weight					
	Reps					
	Weight					
	Reps					
	Weight					

Cardio

Exercise	Calories	Distance	Time

Water Intake _____

Cooldown _____

Feeling ☆ ☆ ☆ ☆ ☆

Notes

Today's Goal _____   Ⓜ Ⓣ Ⓦ Ⓣ Ⓕ ● ●

Focus_____**Date/Time** _____

Stretch ○   **Warm-Up** _____

Strength/Balance/Flexibility Training

Exercise		Set 1	Set 2	Set 3	Set 4	Set 5
	Reps					
	Weight					
	Reps					
	Weight					
	Reps					
	Weight					
	Reps					
	Weight					
	Reps					
	Weight					
	Reps					
	Weight					
	Reps					
	Weight					
	Reps					
	Weight					
	Reps					
	Weight					
	Reps					
	Weight					

Cardio

Exercise	Calories	Distance	Time

Water Intake _____

Cooldown _____

Feeling ☆ ☆ ☆ ☆ ☆

Notes

Today's Goal _____

(M) (T) (W) (T) (F) **S** **S**

Focus_____ Date/Time _____

Stretch ○   Warm-Up _____

Strength/Balance/Flexibility Training

Exercise		Set 1	Set 2	Set 3	Set 4	Set 5
	Reps					
	Weight					
	Reps					
	Weight					
	Reps					
	Weight					
	Reps					
	Weight					
	Reps					
	Weight					
	Reps					
	Weight					
	Reps					
	Weight					
	Reps					
	Weight					
	Reps					
	Weight					
	Reps					
	Weight					

Cardio

Exercise	Calories	Distance	Time

Water Intake _____

Cooldown _____

Feeling ☆ ☆ ☆ ☆ ☆

Notes

Today's Goal _____ Ⓜ Ⓣ Ⓦ Ⓣ Ⓕ 🅢 🅢

Focus_____**Date/Time**_____

Stretch ◯   **Warm-Up** _____

Strength/Balance/Flexibility Training

Exercise		Set 1	Set 2	Set 3	Set 4	Set 5
	Reps					
	Weight					
	Reps					
	Weight					
	Reps					
	Weight					
	Reps					
	Weight					
	Reps					
	Weight					
	Reps					
	Weight					
	Reps					
	Weight					
	Reps					
	Weight					
	Reps					
	Weight					
	Reps					
	Weight					

Cardio

Exercise	Calories	Distance	Time

Water Intake _____

Cooldown _____

Feeling ☆ ☆ ☆ ☆ ☆

Notes

Today's Goal _____ Ⓜ Ⓣ Ⓦ Ⓣ Ⓕ ⚫ ⚫

Focus_____**Date/Time** _____

Stretch ◯   **Warm-Up** _____

Strength/Balance/Flexibility Training

Exercise		Set 1	Set 2	Set 3	Set 4	Set 5
	Reps					
	Weight					
	Reps					
	Weight					
	Reps					
	Weight					
	Reps					
	Weight					
	Reps					
	Weight					
	Reps					
	Weight					
	Reps					
	Weight					
	Reps					
	Weight					
	Reps					
	Weight					
	Reps					
	Weight					

Cardio

Exercise	Calories	Distance	Time

Water Intake _____

Cooldown _____

Feeling ☆ ☆ ☆ ☆ ☆

Notes

Today's Goal _____   Ⓜ Ⓣ Ⓦ Ⓣ Ⓕ ● ●

Focus _____ **Date/Time** _____

Stretch ○   **Warm-Up** _____

Strength/Balance/Flexibility Training

Exercise		Set 1	Set 2	Set 3	Set 4	Set 5
	Reps					
	Weight					
	Reps					
	Weight					
	Reps					
	Weight					
	Reps					
	Weight					
	Reps					
	Weight					
	Reps					
	Weight					
	Reps					
	Weight					
	Reps					
	Weight					
	Reps					
	Weight					
	Reps					
	Weight					

Cardio

Exercise	Calories	Distance	Time

Water Intake _____

Cooldown _____

Feeling ☆ ☆ ☆ ☆ ☆

Notes

Today's Goal _____ Ⓜ Ⓣ Ⓦ Ⓣ Ⓕ ⬤ ⬤

Focus_____ Date/Time _____

Stretch ◯   Warm-Up _____

Strength/Balance/Flexibility Training

Exercise		Set 1	Set 2	Set 3	Set 4	Set 5
	Reps					
	Weight					
	Reps					
	Weight					
	Reps					
	Weight					
	Reps					
	Weight					
	Reps					
	Weight					
	Reps					
	Weight					
	Reps					
	Weight					
	Reps					
	Weight					
	Reps					
	Weight					
	Reps					
	Weight					

Cardio

Exercise	Calories	Distance	Time

Water Intake _____

Cooldown _____

Feeling ☆ ☆ ☆ ☆ ☆

Notes

Today's Goal _____ Ⓜ Ⓣ Ⓦ Ⓣ Ⓕ ⬤ ⬤

Focus_____**Date/Time** _____

Stretch ◯   **Warm-Up** _____

Strength/Balance/Flexibility Training

Exercise		Set 1	Set 2	Set 3	Set 4	Set 5
	Reps					
	Weight					
	Reps					
	Weight					
	Reps					
	Weight					
	Reps					
	Weight					
	Reps					
	Weight					
	Reps					
	Weight					
	Reps					
	Weight					
	Reps					
	Weight					
	Reps					
	Weight					
	Reps					
	Weight					

Cardio

Exercise	Calories	Distance	Time

Water Intake _____

Cooldown _____

Feeling ☆ ☆ ☆ ☆ ☆

Notes

Today's Goal _____ Ⓜ Ⓣ Ⓦ Ⓣ Ⓕ ⬤ ⬤

Focus_____Date/Time _____

Stretch ◯   Warm-Up _____

Strength/Balance/Flexibility Training

Exercise		Set 1	Set 2	Set 3	Set 4	Set 5
	Reps					
	Weight					
	Reps					
	Weight					
	Reps					
	Weight					
	Reps					
	Weight					
	Reps					
	Weight					
	Reps					
	Weight					
	Reps					
	Weight					
	Reps					
	Weight					
	Reps					
	Weight					
	Reps					
	Weight					

Cardio

Exercise	Calories	Distance	Time

Water Intake _____

Cooldown _____

Feeling ☆ ☆ ☆ ☆ ☆

Notes

Today's Goal _____ (M) (T) (W) (T) (F) ● ●

Focus_____ **Date/Time** _____

Stretch ◯   **Warm-Up** _____

Strength/Balance/Flexibility Training

Exercise		Set 1	Set 2	Set 3	Set 4	Set 5
	Reps					
	Weight					
	Reps					
	Weight					
	Reps					
	Weight					
	Reps					
	Weight					
	Reps					
	Weight					
	Reps					
	Weight					
	Reps					
	Weight					
	Reps					
	Weight					
	Reps					
	Weight					
	Reps					
	Weight					

Cardio

Exercise	Calories	Distance	Time

Water Intake _____

Cooldown _____

Feeling ☆ ☆ ☆ ☆ ☆

Notes

Today's Goal _____ Ⓜ Ⓣ Ⓦ Ⓣ Ⓕ ● ●

Focus_____**Date/Time** _____

Stretch ○   **Warm-Up** _____

Strength/Balance/Flexibility Training

Exercise		Set 1	Set 2	Set 3	Set 4	Set 5
	Reps					
	Weight					
	Reps					
	Weight					
	Reps					
	Weight					
	Reps					
	Weight					
	Reps					
	Weight					
	Reps					
	Weight					
	Reps					
	Weight					
	Reps					
	Weight					
	Reps					
	Weight					
	Reps					
	Weight					

Cardio

Exercise	Calories	Distance	Time

Water Intake _____

Cooldown _____

Feeling ☆ ☆ ☆ ☆ ☆

Notes

Today's Goal _____ Ⓜ Ⓣ Ⓦ Ⓣ Ⓕ ● ●

Focus _____ **Date/Time** _____

Stretch ◯   **Warm-Up** _____

Strength/Balance/Flexibility Training

Exercise		Set 1	Set 2	Set 3	Set 4	Set 5
	Reps					
	Weight					
	Reps					
	Weight					
	Reps					
	Weight					
	Reps					
	Weight					
	Reps					
	Weight					
	Reps					
	Weight					
	Reps					
	Weight					
	Reps					
	Weight					
	Reps					
	Weight					
	Reps					
	Weight					

Cardio

Exercise	Calories	Distance	Time

Water Intake _____

Cooldown _____

Feeling ☆ ☆ ☆ ☆ ☆

Notes

Today's Goal _____ (M)(T)(W)(T)(F)(S)(S)

Focus_____Date/Time _____

Stretch ◯   Warm-Up _____

Strength/Balance/Flexibility Training

Exercise		Set 1	Set 2	Set 3	Set 4	Set 5
	Reps					
	Weight					
	Reps					
	Weight					
	Reps					
	Weight					
	Reps					
	Weight					
	Reps					
	Weight					
	Reps					
	Weight					
	Reps					
	Weight					
	Reps					
	Weight					
	Reps					
	Weight					
	Reps					
	Weight					

Cardio

Exercise	Calories	Distance	Time

Water Intake _____

Cooldown _____

Feeling ☆ ☆ ☆ ☆ ☆

Notes

Today's Goal _____ Ⓜ Ⓣ Ⓦ Ⓣ Ⓕ ⬤S ⬤S

Focus _____ Date/Time _____

Stretch ◯   Warm-Up _____

Strength/Balance/Flexibility Training

Exercise		Set 1	Set 2	Set 3	Set 4	Set 5
	Reps					
	Weight					
	Reps					
	Weight					
	Reps					
	Weight					
	Reps					
	Weight					
	Reps					
	Weight					
	Reps					
	Weight					
	Reps					
	Weight					
	Reps					
	Weight					
	Reps					
	Weight					
	Reps					
	Weight					

Cardio

Exercise	Calories	Distance	Time

Water Intake _____

Cooldown _____

Feeling ☆ ☆ ☆ ☆ ☆

Notes

Today's Goal _____ Ⓜ Ⓣ Ⓦ Ⓣ Ⓕ ⬤ ⬤

Focus_____**Date/Time** _____

Stretch ◯   **Warm-Up** _____

Strength/Balance/Flexibility Training

Exercise		Set 1	Set 2	Set 3	Set 4	Set 5
	Reps					
	Weight					
	Reps					
	Weight					
	Reps					
	Weight					
	Reps					
	Weight					
	Reps					
	Weight					
	Reps					
	Weight					
	Reps					
	Weight					
	Reps					
	Weight					
	Reps					
	Weight					
	Reps					
	Weight					

Cardio

Exercise	Calories	Distance	Time

Water Intake _____

Cooldown _____

Feeling ☆ ☆ ☆ ☆ ☆

Notes

Today's Goal _____   (M) (T) (W) (T) (F) ● ●

Focus _____ **Date/Time** _____

Stretch ○   **Warm-Up** _____

Strength/Balance/Flexibility Training

Exercise		Set 1	Set 2	Set 3	Set 4	Set 5
	Reps					
	Weight					
	Reps					
	Weight					
	Reps					
	Weight					
	Reps					
	Weight					
	Reps					
	Weight					
	Reps					
	Weight					
	Reps					
	Weight					
	Reps					
	Weight					
	Reps					
	Weight					
	Reps					
	Weight					

Cardio

Exercise	Calories	Distance	Time

Water Intake _____

Cooldown _____

Feeling ☆ ☆ ☆ ☆ ☆

Notes

Today's Goal _____ Ⓜ Ⓣ Ⓦ Ⓣ Ⓕ ● ●

Focus_____**Date/Time** _____

Stretch ◯   **Warm-Up** _____

Strength/Balance/Flexibility Training

Exercise		Set 1	Set 2	Set 3	Set 4	Set 5
	Reps					
	Weight					
	Reps					
	Weight					
	Reps					
	Weight					
	Reps					
	Weight					
	Reps					
	Weight					
	Reps					
	Weight					
	Reps					
	Weight					
	Reps					
	Weight					
	Reps					
	Weight					
	Reps					
	Weight					

Cardio

Exercise	Calories	Distance	Time

Water Intake _____

Cooldown _____

Feeling ☆ ☆ ☆ ☆ ☆

Notes

Today's Goal _____ Ⓜ Ⓣ Ⓦ Ⓣ Ⓕ ⬤ ⬤

Focus_____ Date/Time _____

Stretch ◯　　　Warm-Up _____

Strength/Balance/Flexibility Training

Exercise		Set 1	Set 2	Set 3	Set 4	Set 5
	Reps					
	Weight					
	Reps					
	Weight					
	Reps					
	Weight					
	Reps					
	Weight					
	Reps					
	Weight					
	Reps					
	Weight					
	Reps					
	Weight					
	Reps					
	Weight					
	Reps					
	Weight					
	Reps					
	Weight					

Cardio

Exercise	Calories	Distance	Time

Water Intake _____

Cooldown _____

Feeling ☆ ☆ ☆ ☆ ☆

Notes

Today's Goal _____ (M) (T) (W) (T) (F) ● ●

Focus_____**Date/Time**_____

Stretch ○   **Warm-Up** _____

Strength/Balance/Flexibility Training

Exercise		Set 1	Set 2	Set 3	Set 4	Set 5
	Reps					
	Weight					
	Reps					
	Weight					
	Reps					
	Weight					
	Reps					
	Weight					
	Reps					
	Weight					
	Reps					
	Weight					
	Reps					
	Weight					
	Reps					
	Weight					
	Reps					
	Weight					
	Reps					
	Weight					

Cardio

Exercise	Calories	Distance	Time

Water Intake _____

Cooldown _____

Feeling ☆ ☆ ☆ ☆ ☆

Notes

Today's Goal _____ Ⓜ Ⓣ Ⓦ Ⓣ Ⓕ ⬤S ⬤S

Focus _____ **Date/Time** _____

Stretch ◯   **Warm-Up** _____

Strength/Balance/Flexibility Training

Exercise		Set 1	Set 2	Set 3	Set 4	Set 5
	Reps					
	Weight					
	Reps					
	Weight					
	Reps					
	Weight					
	Reps					
	Weight					
	Reps					
	Weight					
	Reps					
	Weight					
	Reps					
	Weight					
	Reps					
	Weight					
	Reps					
	Weight					
	Reps					
	Weight					

Cardio

Exercise	Calories	Distance	Time

Water Intake _____

Cooldown _____

Feeling ☆ ☆ ☆ ☆ ☆

Notes

Today's Goal _____ Ⓜ Ⓣ Ⓦ Ⓣ Ⓕ ⬤ ⬤

Focus_____**Date/Time**_____

Stretch ◯   **Warm-Up** _____

Strength/Balance/Flexibility Training

Exercise		Set 1	Set 2	Set 3	Set 4	Set 5
	Reps					
	Weight					
	Reps					
	Weight					
	Reps					
	Weight					
	Reps					
	Weight					
	Reps					
	Weight					
	Reps					
	Weight					
	Reps					
	Weight					
	Reps					
	Weight					
	Reps					
	Weight					
	Reps					
	Weight					

Cardio

Exercise	Calories	Distance	Time

Water Intake _____

Cooldown _____

Feeling ☆ ☆ ☆ ☆ ☆

Notes

Today's Goal _____ Ⓜ Ⓣ Ⓦ Ⓣ Ⓕ **Ⓢ** **Ⓢ**

Focus _____ **Date/Time** _____

Stretch ◯　　**Warm-Up** _____

Strength/Balance/Flexibility Training

Exercise		Set 1	Set 2	Set 3	Set 4	Set 5
	Reps					
	Weight					
	Reps					
	Weight					
	Reps					
	Weight					
	Reps					
	Weight					
	Reps					
	Weight					
	Reps					
	Weight					
	Reps					
	Weight					
	Reps					
	Weight					
	Reps					
	Weight					
	Reps					
	Weight					

Cardio

Exercise	Calories	Distance	Time

Water Intake _____

Cooldown _____

Feeling ☆☆☆☆☆

Notes

Today's Goal _____ Ⓜ Ⓣ Ⓦ Ⓣ Ⓕ ⬤ ⬤

Focus_____Date/Time _____

Stretch ○   Warm-Up _____

Strength/Balance/Flexibility Training

Exercise		Set 1	Set 2	Set 3	Set 4	Set 5
	Reps					
	Weight					
	Reps					
	Weight					
	Reps					
	Weight					
	Reps					
	Weight					
	Reps					
	Weight					
	Reps					
	Weight					
	Reps					
	Weight					
	Reps					
	Weight					
	Reps					
	Weight					
	Reps					
	Weight					

Cardio

Exercise	Calories	Distance	Time

Water Intake _____

Cooldown _____

Feeling ☆ ☆ ☆ ☆ ☆

Notes

Today's Goal _____   Ⓜ Ⓣ Ⓦ Ⓣ Ⓕ ⬤ ⬤

Focus_____**Date/Time** _____

Stretch ○   **Warm-Up** _____

Strength/Balance/Flexibility Training

Exercise		Set 1	Set 2	Set 3	Set 4	Set 5
	Reps					
	Weight					
	Reps					
	Weight					
	Reps					
	Weight					
	Reps					
	Weight					
	Reps					
	Weight					
	Reps					
	Weight					
	Reps					
	Weight					
	Reps					
	Weight					
	Reps					
	Weight					
	Reps					
	Weight					

Cardio

Exercise	Calories	Distance	Time

Water Intake _____

Cooldown _____

Feeling ☆ ☆ ☆ ☆ ☆

Notes

Today's Goal _____ Ⓜ Ⓣ Ⓦ Ⓣ Ⓕ ⚫ ⚫

Focus_____**Date/Time**_____

Stretch ◯   **Warm-Up** _____

Strength/Balance/Flexibility Training

Exercise		Set 1	Set 2	Set 3	Set 4	Set 5
	Reps					
	Weight					
	Reps					
	Weight					
	Reps					
	Weight					
	Reps					
	Weight					
	Reps					
	Weight					
	Reps					
	Weight					
	Reps					
	Weight					
	Reps					
	Weight					
	Reps					
	Weight					
	Reps					
	Weight					

Cardio

Exercise	Calories	Distance	Time

Water Intake _____

Cooldown _____

Feeling ☆ ☆ ☆ ☆ ☆

Notes

Today's Goal _____ Ⓜ Ⓣ Ⓦ Ⓣ Ⓕ Ⓢ Ⓢ

Focus_____ **Date/Time** _____

Stretch ◯   **Warm-Up** _____

Strength/Balance/Flexibility Training

Exercise		Set 1	Set 2	Set 3	Set 4	Set 5
	Reps					
	Weight					
	Reps					
	Weight					
	Reps					
	Weight					
	Reps					
	Weight					
	Reps					
	Weight					
	Reps					
	Weight					
	Reps					
	Weight					
	Reps					
	Weight					
	Reps					
	Weight					
	Reps					
	Weight					

Cardio

Exercise	Calories	Distance	Time

Water Intake _____

Cooldown _____

Feeling ☆ ☆ ☆ ☆ ☆

Notes

Today's Goal _____   (M) (T) (W) (T) (F) (S) (S)

Focus_____ Date/Time _____

Stretch ◯   Warm-Up _____

Strength/Balance/Flexibility Training

Exercise		Set 1	Set 2	Set 3	Set 4	Set 5
	Reps					
	Weight					
	Reps					
	Weight					
	Reps					
	Weight					
	Reps					
	Weight					
	Reps					
	Weight					
	Reps					
	Weight					
	Reps					
	Weight					
	Reps					
	Weight					
	Reps					
	Weight					
	Reps					
	Weight					

Cardio

Exercise	Calories	Distance	Time

Water Intake _____

Cooldown _____

Feeling ☆ ☆ ☆ ☆ ☆

Notes

Today's Goal _____

(M) (T) (W) (T) (F) (S) (S)

Focus_____**Date/Time** _____

Stretch ◯   **Warm-Up** _____

Strength/Balance/Flexibility Training

Exercise		Set 1	Set 2	Set 3	Set 4	Set 5
	Reps					
	Weight					
	Reps					
	Weight					
	Reps					
	Weight					
	Reps					
	Weight					
	Reps					
	Weight					
	Reps					
	Weight					
	Reps					
	Weight					
	Reps					
	Weight					
	Reps					
	Weight					
	Reps					
	Weight					

Cardio

Exercise	Calories	Distance	Time

Water Intake _____

Cooldown _____

Feeling ☆ ☆ ☆ ☆ ☆

Notes

Today's Goal _____ Ⓜ Ⓣ Ⓦ Ⓣ Ⓕ ● ●

Focus_____ **Date/Time** _____

Stretch ◯   **Warm-Up** _____

Strength/Balance/Flexibility Training

Exercise		Set 1	Set 2	Set 3	Set 4	Set 5
	Reps					
	Weight					
	Reps					
	Weight					
	Reps					
	Weight					
	Reps					
	Weight					
	Reps					
	Weight					
	Reps					
	Weight					
	Reps					
	Weight					
	Reps					
	Weight					
	Reps					
	Weight					
	Reps					
	Weight					

Cardio

Exercise	Calories	Distance	Time

Water Intake _____

Cooldown _____

Feeling ☆ ☆ ☆ ☆ ☆

Notes

Today's Goal _____ Ⓜ Ⓣ Ⓦ Ⓣ Ⓕ ⚫ ⚫

Focus_____ **Date/Time** _____

Stretch ◯   **Warm-Up** _____

Strength/Balance/Flexibility Training

Exercise		Set 1	Set 2	Set 3	Set 4	Set 5
	Reps					
	Weight					
	Reps					
	Weight					
	Reps					
	Weight					
	Reps					
	Weight					
	Reps					
	Weight					
	Reps					
	Weight					
	Reps					
	Weight					
	Reps					
	Weight					
	Reps					
	Weight					
	Reps					
	Weight					

Cardio

Exercise	Calories	Distance	Time

Water Intake _____

Cooldown _____

Feeling ☆ ☆ ☆ ☆ ☆

Notes

Today's Goal _____ Ⓜ Ⓣ Ⓦ Ⓣ Ⓕ ⬤ ⬤

Focus_____ **Date/Time** _____

Stretch ◯　　**Warm-Up** _____

Strength/Balance/Flexibility Training

Exercise		Set 1	Set 2	Set 3	Set 4	Set 5
	Reps					
	Weight					
	Reps					
	Weight					
	Reps					
	Weight					
	Reps					
	Weight					
	Reps					
	Weight					
	Reps					
	Weight					
	Reps					
	Weight					
	Reps					
	Weight					
	Reps					
	Weight					
	Reps					
	Weight					

Cardio

Exercise	Calories	Distance	Time

Water Intake _____

Cooldown _____

Feeling ☆ ☆ ☆ ☆ ☆

Notes

Today's Goal _____   Ⓜ Ⓣ Ⓦ Ⓣ Ⓕ ⚫ ⚫

Focus_____**Date/Time** _____

Stretch ◯   **Warm-Up** _____

Strength/Balance/Flexibility Training

Exercise		Set 1	Set 2	Set 3	Set 4	Set 5
	Reps					
	Weight					
	Reps					
	Weight					
	Reps					
	Weight					
	Reps					
	Weight					
	Reps					
	Weight					
	Reps					
	Weight					
	Reps					
	Weight					
	Reps					
	Weight					
	Reps					
	Weight					
	Reps					
	Weight					

Cardio

Exercise	Calories	Distance	Time

Water Intake _____

Cooldown _____

Feeling ☆ ☆ ☆ ☆ ☆

Notes

Today's Goal _____   Ⓜ Ⓣ Ⓦ Ⓣ Ⓕ ● ●

Focus_____Date/Time _____

Stretch ◯   Warm-Up _____

Strength/Balance/Flexibility Training

Exercise		Set 1	Set 2	Set 3	Set 4	Set 5
	Reps					
	Weight					
	Reps					
	Weight					
	Reps					
	Weight					
	Reps					
	Weight					
	Reps					
	Weight					
	Reps					
	Weight					
	Reps					
	Weight					
	Reps					
	Weight					
	Reps					
	Weight					
	Reps					
	Weight					

Cardio

Exercise	Calories	Distance	Time

Water Intake _____

Cooldown _____

Feeling ☆ ☆ ☆ ☆ ☆

Notes

Today's Goal _____ Ⓜ Ⓣ Ⓦ Ⓣ Ⓕ ⬤ ⬤

Focus_____ **Date/Time** _____

Stretch ◯   **Warm-Up** _____

Strength/Balance/Flexibility Training

Exercise		Set 1	Set 2	Set 3	Set 4	Set 5
	Reps					
	Weight					
	Reps					
	Weight					
	Reps					
	Weight					
	Reps					
	Weight					
	Reps					
	Weight					
	Reps					
	Weight					
	Reps					
	Weight					
	Reps					
	Weight					
	Reps					
	Weight					
	Reps					
	Weight					
	Reps					
	Weight					
	Reps					
	Weight					

Cardio

Exercise	Calories	Distance	Time

Water Intake _____

Cooldown _____

Feeling ☆ ☆ ☆ ☆ ☆

Notes

Today's Goal _____ Ⓜ Ⓣ Ⓦ Ⓣ Ⓕ ●S ●S

Focus_____**Date/Time**_____

Stretch ◯   **Warm-Up** _____

Strength/Balance/Flexibility Training

Exercise		Set 1	Set 2	Set 3	Set 4	Set 5
	Reps					
	Weight					
	Reps					
	Weight					
	Reps					
	Weight					
	Reps					
	Weight					
	Reps					
	Weight					
	Reps					
	Weight					
	Reps					
	Weight					
	Reps					
	Weight					
	Reps					
	Weight					
	Reps					
	Weight					

Cardio

Exercise	Calories	Distance	Time

Water Intake _____

Cooldown _____

Feeling ☆ ☆ ☆ ☆ ☆

Notes

Today's Goal _____

(M) (T) (W) (T) (F) ● ●

Focus _____ Date/Time _____

Stretch ○   Warm-Up _____

Strength/Balance/Flexibility Training

Exercise		Set 1	Set 2	Set 3	Set 4	Set 5
	Reps					
	Weight					
	Reps					
	Weight					
	Reps					
	Weight					
	Reps					
	Weight					
	Reps					
	Weight					
	Reps					
	Weight					
	Reps					
	Weight					
	Reps					
	Weight					
	Reps					
	Weight					
	Reps					
	Weight					

Cardio

Exercise	Calories	Distance	Time

Water Intake _____

Cooldown _____

Feeling ☆ ☆ ☆ ☆ ☆

Notes

Today's Goal _____ Ⓜ Ⓣ Ⓦ Ⓣ Ⓕ ● ●

Focus_____**Date/Time**_____

Stretch ○   **Warm-Up** _____

Strength/Balance/Flexibility Training

Exercise		Set 1	Set 2	Set 3	Set 4	Set 5
	Reps					
	Weight					
	Reps					
	Weight					
	Reps					
	Weight					
	Reps					
	Weight					
	Reps					
	Weight					
	Reps					
	Weight					
	Reps					
	Weight					
	Reps					
	Weight					
	Reps					
	Weight					
	Reps					
	Weight					

Cardio

Exercise	Calories	Distance	Time

Water Intake _____

Cooldown _____

Feeling ☆ ☆ ☆ ☆ ☆

Notes

Today's Goal _____

(M) (T) (W) (T) (F) (S) (S)

Focus _____ **Date/Time** _____

Stretch ○   **Warm-Up** _____

Strength/Balance/Flexibility Training

Exercise		Set 1	Set 2	Set 3	Set 4	Set 5
	Reps					
	Weight					
	Reps					
	Weight					
	Reps					
	Weight					
	Reps					
	Weight					
	Reps					
	Weight					
	Reps					
	Weight					
	Reps					
	Weight					
	Reps					
	Weight					
	Reps					
	Weight					
	Reps					
	Weight					

Cardio

Exercise	Calories	Distance	Time

Water Intake _____

Cooldown _____

Feeling ☆ ☆ ☆ ☆ ☆

Notes

Today's Goal _____

(M) (T) (W) (T) (F) **S** **S**

Focus_____**Date/Time** _____

Stretch ◯   **Warm-Up** _____

Strength/Balance/Flexibility Training

Exercise		Set 1	Set 2	Set 3	Set 4	Set 5
	Reps					
	Weight					
	Reps					
	Weight					
	Reps					
	Weight					
	Reps					
	Weight					
	Reps					
	Weight					
	Reps					
	Weight					
	Reps					
	Weight					
	Reps					
	Weight					
	Reps					
	Weight					
	Reps					
	Weight					

Cardio

Exercise	Calories	Distance	Time

Water Intake _____

Cooldown _____

Feeling ☆ ☆ ☆ ☆ ☆

Notes

Today's Goal _____ Ⓜ Ⓣ Ⓦ Ⓣ Ⓕ ⓢ ⓢ

Focus_____**Date/Time** _____

Stretch ◯   **Warm-Up** _____

Strength/Balance/Flexibility Training

Exercise		Set 1	Set 2	Set 3	Set 4	Set 5
	Reps					
	Weight					
	Reps					
	Weight					
	Reps					
	Weight					
	Reps					
	Weight					
	Reps					
	Weight					
	Reps					
	Weight					
	Reps					
	Weight					
	Reps					
	Weight					
	Reps					
	Weight					
	Reps					
	Weight					

Cardio

Exercise	Calories	Distance	Time

Water Intake _____

Cooldown _____

Feeling ☆ ☆ ☆ ☆ ☆

Notes

Today's Goal _____ Ⓜ Ⓣ Ⓦ Ⓣ Ⓕ **Ⓢ** **Ⓢ**

Focus_____**Date/Time**_____

Stretch ○   **Warm-Up** _____

Strength/Balance/Flexibility Training

Exercise		Set 1	Set 2	Set 3	Set 4	Set 5
	Reps					
	Weight					
	Reps					
	Weight					
	Reps					
	Weight					
	Reps					
	Weight					
	Reps					
	Weight					
	Reps					
	Weight					
	Reps					
	Weight					
	Reps					
	Weight					
	Reps					
	Weight					
	Reps					
	Weight					

Cardio

Exercise	Calories	Distance	Time

Water Intake _____

Cooldown _____

Feeling ☆ ☆ ☆ ☆ ☆

Notes

Today's Goal _____   (M) (T) (W) (T) (F) (S) (S)

Focus_____**Date/Time** _____

Stretch ◯   **Warm-Up** _____

Strength/Balance/Flexibility Training

Exercise		Set 1	Set 2	Set 3	Set 4	Set 5
	Reps					
	Weight					
	Reps					
	Weight					
	Reps					
	Weight					
	Reps					
	Weight					
	Reps					
	Weight					
	Reps					
	Weight					
	Reps					
	Weight					
	Reps					
	Weight					
	Reps					
	Weight					
	Reps					
	Weight					

Cardio

Exercise	Calories	Distance	Time

Water Intake _____

Cooldown _____

Feeling ☆ ☆ ☆ ☆ ☆

Notes

Today's Goal _____ Ⓜ Ⓣ Ⓦ Ⓣ Ⓕ ⬤ ⬤

Focus_____ Date/Time _____

Stretch ◯   Warm-Up _____

Strength/Balance/Flexibility Training

Exercise		Set 1	Set 2	Set 3	Set 4	Set 5
	Reps					
	Weight					
	Reps					
	Weight					
	Reps					
	Weight					
	Reps					
	Weight					
	Reps					
	Weight					
	Reps					
	Weight					
	Reps					
	Weight					
	Reps					
	Weight					
	Reps					
	Weight					
	Reps					
	Weight					

Cardio

Exercise	Calories	Distance	Time

Water Intake _____

Cooldown _____

Feeling ☆ ☆ ☆ ☆ ☆

Notes

Today's Goal _____ Ⓜ Ⓣ Ⓦ Ⓣ Ⓕ ⚫ ⚫

Focus_____**Date/Time** _____

Stretch ◯   **Warm-Up** _____

Strength/Balance/Flexibility Training

Exercise		Set 1	Set 2	Set 3	Set 4	Set 5
	Reps					
	Weight					
	Reps					
	Weight					
	Reps					
	Weight					
	Reps					
	Weight					
	Reps					
	Weight					
	Reps					
	Weight					
	Reps					
	Weight					
	Reps					
	Weight					
	Reps					
	Weight					
	Reps					
	Weight					

Cardio

Exercise	Calories	Distance	Time

Water Intake _____

Cooldown _____

Feeling ☆ ☆ ☆ ☆ ☆

Notes

Today's Goal _____ Ⓜ Ⓣ Ⓦ Ⓣ Ⓕ ● ●

Focus_____**Date/Time** _____

Stretch ○   **Warm-Up** _____

Strength/Balance/Flexibility Training

Exercise		Set 1	Set 2	Set 3	Set 4	Set 5
	Reps					
	Weight					
	Reps					
	Weight					
	Reps					
	Weight					
	Reps					
	Weight					
	Reps					
	Weight					
	Reps					
	Weight					
	Reps					
	Weight					
	Reps					
	Weight					
	Reps					
	Weight					
	Reps					
	Weight					

Cardio

Exercise	Calories	Distance	Time

Water Intake _____

Cooldown _____

Feeling ☆ ☆ ☆ ☆ ☆

Notes

Today's Goal _____   Ⓜ Ⓣ Ⓦ Ⓣ Ⓕ ⬤ ⬤

Focus_____**Date/Time** _____

Stretch ◯   **Warm-Up** _____

Strength/Balance/Flexibility Training

Exercise		Set 1	Set 2	Set 3	Set 4	Set 5
	Reps					
	Weight					
	Reps					
	Weight					
	Reps					
	Weight					
	Reps					
	Weight					
	Reps					
	Weight					
	Reps					
	Weight					
	Reps					
	Weight					
	Reps					
	Weight					
	Reps					
	Weight					
	Reps					
	Weight					

Cardio

Exercise	Calories	Distance	Time

Water Intake _____

Cooldown _____

Feeling ☆ ☆ ☆ ☆ ☆

Notes

Today's Goal _____ Ⓜ Ⓣ Ⓦ Ⓣ Ⓕ 🅢 🅢

Focus_____**Date/Time** _____

Stretch ◯   **Warm-Up** _____

Strength/Balance/Flexibility Training

Exercise		Set 1	Set 2	Set 3	Set 4	Set 5
	Reps					
	Weight					
	Reps					
	Weight					
	Reps					
	Weight					
	Reps					
	Weight					
	Reps					
	Weight					
	Reps					
	Weight					
	Reps					
	Weight					
	Reps					
	Weight					
	Reps					
	Weight					
	Reps					
	Weight					

Cardio

Exercise	Calories	Distance	Time

Water Intake _____

Cooldown _____

Feeling ☆ ☆ ☆ ☆ ☆

Notes

Today's Goal _____ Ⓜ Ⓣ Ⓦ Ⓣ Ⓕ ⬤ ⬤

Focus_____Date/Time _____

Stretch ◯   Warm-Up _____

Strength/Balance/Flexibility Training

Exercise		Set 1	Set 2	Set 3	Set 4	Set 5
	Reps					
	Weight					
	Reps					
	Weight					
	Reps					
	Weight					
	Reps					
	Weight					
	Reps					
	Weight					
	Reps					
	Weight					
	Reps					
	Weight					
	Reps					
	Weight					
	Reps					
	Weight					
	Reps					
	Weight					

Cardio

Exercise	Calories	Distance	Time

Water Intake _____

Cooldown _____

Feeling ☆ ☆ ☆ ☆ ☆

Notes

Today's Goal _____ Ⓜ Ⓣ Ⓦ Ⓣ Ⓕ ⬤ ⬤

Focus _____ **Date/Time** _____

Stretch ◯   **Warm-Up** _____

Strength/Balance/Flexibility Training

Exercise		Set 1	Set 2	Set 3	Set 4	Set 5
	Reps					
	Weight					
	Reps					
	Weight					
	Reps					
	Weight					
	Reps					
	Weight					
	Reps					
	Weight					
	Reps					
	Weight					
	Reps					
	Weight					
	Reps					
	Weight					
	Reps					
	Weight					
	Reps					
	Weight					

Cardio

Exercise	Calories	Distance	Time

Water Intake _____

Cooldown _____

Feeling ☆ ☆ ☆ ☆ ☆

Notes

Today's Goal _____ Ⓜ ⓉⓌⓉⒻ ⬤⬤

Focus_____**Date/Time**_____

Stretch ◯   **Warm-Up** _____

Strength/Balance/Flexibility Training

Exercise		Set 1	Set 2	Set 3	Set 4	Set 5
	Reps					
	Weight					
	Reps					
	Weight					
	Reps					
	Weight					
	Reps					
	Weight					
	Reps					
	Weight					
	Reps					
	Weight					
	Reps					
	Weight					
	Reps					
	Weight					
	Reps					
	Weight					
	Reps					
	Weight					

Cardio

Exercise	Calories	Distance	Time

Water Intake _____

Cooldown _____

Feeling ☆ ☆ ☆ ☆ ☆

Notes

Today's Goal _____   Ⓜ Ⓣ Ⓦ Ⓣ Ⓕ ⬤ ⬤

Focus_____**Date/Time**_____

Stretch ◯   **Warm-Up** _____

Strength/Balance/Flexibility Training

Exercise		Set 1	Set 2	Set 3	Set 4	Set 5
	Reps					
	Weight					
	Reps					
	Weight					
	Reps					
	Weight					
	Reps					
	Weight					
	Reps					
	Weight					
	Reps					
	Weight					
	Reps					
	Weight					
	Reps					
	Weight					
	Reps					
	Weight					
	Reps					
	Weight					

Cardio

Exercise	Calories	Distance	Time

Water Intake _____

Cooldown _____

Feeling ☆ ☆ ☆ ☆ ☆

Notes

Today's Goal _____ Ⓜ Ⓣ Ⓦ Ⓣ Ⓕ ⬤ ⬤

Focus _____ Date/Time _____

Stretch ○   Warm-Up _____

Strength/Balance/Flexibility Training

Exercise		Set 1	Set 2	Set 3	Set 4	Set 5
	Reps					
	Weight					
	Reps					
	Weight					
	Reps					
	Weight					
	Reps					
	Weight					
	Reps					
	Weight					
	Reps					
	Weight					
	Reps					
	Weight					
	Reps					
	Weight					
	Reps					
	Weight					
	Reps					
	Weight					

Cardio

Exercise	Calories	Distance	Time

Water Intake _____

Cooldown _____

Feeling ☆ ☆ ☆ ☆ ☆

Notes

Today's Goal _____ Ⓜ Ⓣ Ⓦ Ⓣ Ⓕ 🅢 🅢

Focus_____**Date/Time**_____

Stretch ◯   **Warm-Up** _____

Strength/Balance/Flexibility Training

Exercise		Set 1	Set 2	Set 3	Set 4	Set 5
	Reps					
	Weight					
	Reps					
	Weight					
	Reps					
	Weight					
	Reps					
	Weight					
	Reps					
	Weight					
	Reps					
	Weight					
	Reps					
	Weight					
	Reps					
	Weight					
	Reps					
	Weight					
	Reps					
	Weight					

Cardio

Exercise	Calories	Distance	Time

Water Intake _____

Cooldown _____

Feeling ☆ ☆ ☆ ☆ ☆

Notes

Today's Goal _____ Ⓜ Ⓣ Ⓦ Ⓣ Ⓕ ⬤ ⬤

Focus _____ Date/Time _____

Stretch ◯   **Warm-Up** _____

Strength/Balance/Flexibility Training

Exercise		Set 1	Set 2	Set 3	Set 4	Set 5
	Reps					
	Weight					
	Reps					
	Weight					
	Reps					
	Weight					
	Reps					
	Weight					
	Reps					
	Weight					
	Reps					
	Weight					
	Reps					
	Weight					
	Reps					
	Weight					
	Reps					
	Weight					
	Reps					
	Weight					

Cardio

Exercise	Calories	Distance	Time

Water Intake _____

Cooldown _____

Feeling ☆ ☆ ☆ ☆ ☆

Notes

Today's Goal _____ Ⓜ Ⓣ Ⓦ Ⓣ Ⓕ ⚫ ⚫

Focus_____**Date/Time**_____

Stretch ◯   **Warm-Up** _____

Strength/Balance/Flexibility Training

Exercise		Set 1	Set 2	Set 3	Set 4	Set 5
	Reps					
	Weight					
	Reps					
	Weight					
	Reps					
	Weight					
	Reps					
	Weight					
	Reps					
	Weight					
	Reps					
	Weight					
	Reps					
	Weight					
	Reps					
	Weight					
	Reps					
	Weight					
	Reps					
	Weight					

Cardio

Exercise	Calories	Distance	Time

Water Intake _____

Cooldown _____

Feeling ☆ ☆ ☆ ☆ ☆

Notes

_____

Today's Goal _____ Ⓜ Ⓣ Ⓦ Ⓣ Ⓕ **Ⓢ** **Ⓢ**

Focus_____ **Date/Time** _____

Stretch ◯   **Warm-Up** _____

Strength/Balance/Flexibility Training

Exercise		Set 1	Set 2	Set 3	Set 4	Set 5
	Reps					
	Weight					
	Reps					
	Weight					
	Reps					
	Weight					
	Reps					
	Weight					
	Reps					
	Weight					
	Reps					
	Weight					
	Reps					
	Weight					
	Reps					
	Weight					
	Reps					
	Weight					
	Reps					
	Weight					

Cardio

Exercise	Calories	Distance	Time

Water Intake _____

Cooldown _____

Feeling ☆ ☆ ☆ ☆ ☆

Notes

Today's Goal _____ Ⓜ Ⓣ Ⓦ Ⓣ Ⓕ ⚫ ⚫

Focus_____**Date/Time** _____

Stretch ◯   **Warm-Up** _____

Strength/Balance/Flexibility Training

Exercise		Set 1	Set 2	Set 3	Set 4	Set 5
	Reps					
	Weight					
	Reps					
	Weight					
	Reps					
	Weight					
	Reps					
	Weight					
	Reps					
	Weight					
	Reps					
	Weight					
	Reps					
	Weight					
	Reps					
	Weight					
	Reps					
	Weight					
	Reps					
	Weight					

Cardio

Exercise	Calories	Distance	Time

Water Intake _____

Cooldown _____

Feeling ☆ ☆ ☆ ☆ ☆

Notes

Today's Goal _____ Ⓜ Ⓣ Ⓦ Ⓣ Ⓕ ⚫ ⚫

Focus_____ **Date/Time** _____

Stretch ◯   **Warm-Up** _____

Strength/Balance/Flexibility Training

Exercise		Set 1	Set 2	Set 3	Set 4	Set 5
	Reps					
	Weight					
	Reps					
	Weight					
	Reps					
	Weight					
	Reps					
	Weight					
	Reps					
	Weight					
	Reps					
	Weight					
	Reps					
	Weight					
	Reps					
	Weight					
	Reps					
	Weight					
	Reps					
	Weight					

Cardio

Exercise	Calories	Distance	Time

Water Intake _____

Cooldown _____

Feeling ☆ ☆ ☆ ☆ ☆

Notes

Today's Goal _____   (M) (T) (W) (T) (F) **(S) (S)**

Focus_____**Date/Time** _____

Stretch ○   **Warm-Up** _____

Strength/Balance/Flexibility Training

Exercise		Set 1	Set 2	Set 3	Set 4	Set 5
	Reps					
	Weight					
	Reps					
	Weight					
	Reps					
	Weight					
	Reps					
	Weight					
	Reps					
	Weight					
	Reps					
	Weight					
	Reps					
	Weight					
	Reps					
	Weight					
	Reps					
	Weight					
	Reps					
	Weight					

Cardio

Exercise	Calories	Distance	Time

Water Intake _____

Cooldown _____

Feeling ☆ ☆ ☆ ☆ ☆

Notes
_____

Today's Goal _____ Ⓜ Ⓣ Ⓦ Ⓣ Ⓕ Ⓢ Ⓢ

Focus _____ Date/Time _____

Stretch ◯   Warm-Up _____

Strength/Balance/Flexibility Training

Exercise		Set 1	Set 2	Set 3	Set 4	Set 5
	Reps					
	Weight					
	Reps					
	Weight					
	Reps					
	Weight					
	Reps					
	Weight					
	Reps					
	Weight					
	Reps					
	Weight					
	Reps					
	Weight					
	Reps					
	Weight					
	Reps					
	Weight					
	Reps					
	Weight					

Cardio

Exercise	Calories	Distance	Time

Water Intake _____

Cooldown _____

Feeling ☆ ☆ ☆ ☆ ☆

Notes

Today's Goal _____   (M)(T)(W)(T)(F)(S)(S)

Focus_____**Date/Time** _____

Stretch ◯   **Warm-Up** _____

Strength/Balance/Flexibility Training

Exercise		Set 1	Set 2	Set 3	Set 4	Set 5
	Reps					
	Weight					
	Reps					
	Weight					
	Reps					
	Weight					
	Reps					
	Weight					
	Reps					
	Weight					
	Reps					
	Weight					
	Reps					
	Weight					
	Reps					
	Weight					
	Reps					
	Weight					
	Reps					
	Weight					

Cardio

Exercise	Calories	Distance	Time

Water Intake _____

Cooldown _____

Feeling ☆ ☆ ☆ ☆ ☆

Notes

Today's Goal _____   (M) (T) (W) (T) (F) (S) (S)

Focus_____Date/Time _____

Stretch ◯   Warm-Up _____

Strength/Balance/Flexibility Training

Exercise		Set 1	Set 2	Set 3	Set 4	Set 5
	Reps					
	Weight					
	Reps					
	Weight					
	Reps					
	Weight					
	Reps					
	Weight					
	Reps					
	Weight					
	Reps					
	Weight					
	Reps					
	Weight					
	Reps					
	Weight					
	Reps					
	Weight					
	Reps					
	Weight					

Cardio

Exercise	Calories	Distance	Time

Water Intake _____

Cooldown _____

Feeling ☆ ☆ ☆ ☆ ☆

Notes

Today's Goal _____ Ⓜ Ⓣ Ⓦ Ⓣ Ⓕ ⬤ ⬤

Focus_____**Date/Time** _____

Stretch ◯   **Warm-Up** _____

Strength/Balance/Flexibility Training

Exercise		Set 1	Set 2	Set 3	Set 4	Set 5
	Reps					
	Weight					
	Reps					
	Weight					
	Reps					
	Weight					
	Reps					
	Weight					
	Reps					
	Weight					
	Reps					
	Weight					
	Reps					
	Weight					
	Reps					
	Weight					
	Reps					
	Weight					
	Reps					
	Weight					

Cardio

Exercise	Calories	Distance	Time

Water Intake _____

Cooldown _____

Feeling ☆ ☆ ☆ ☆ ☆

Notes

Today's Goal _____

(M) (T) (W) (T) (F) (S) (S)

Focus _____ **Date/Time** _____

Stretch ◯   **Warm-Up** _____

Strength/Balance/Flexibility Training

Exercise		Set 1	Set 2	Set 3	Set 4	Set 5
	Reps					
	Weight					
	Reps					
	Weight					
	Reps					
	Weight					
	Reps					
	Weight					
	Reps					
	Weight					
	Reps					
	Weight					
	Reps					
	Weight					
	Reps					
	Weight					
	Reps					
	Weight					
	Reps					
	Weight					

Cardio

Exercise	Calories	Distance	Time

Water Intake _____

Cooldown _____

Feeling ☆ ☆ ☆ ☆ ☆

Notes

Today's Goal _____ Ⓜ Ⓣ Ⓦ Ⓣ Ⓕ ⚫ ⚫

Focus_____**Date/Time** _____

Stretch ◯   **Warm-Up** _____

Strength/Balance/Flexibility Training

Exercise		Set 1	Set 2	Set 3	Set 4	Set 5
	Reps					
	Weight					
	Reps					
	Weight					
	Reps					
	Weight					
	Reps					
	Weight					
	Reps					
	Weight					
	Reps					
	Weight					
	Reps					
	Weight					
	Reps					
	Weight					
	Reps					
	Weight					
	Reps					
	Weight					

Cardio

Exercise	Calories	Distance	Time

Water Intake _____

Cooldown _____

Feeling ☆ ☆ ☆ ☆ ☆

Notes
_____

Today's Goal _____

(M) (T) (W) (T) (F) ● ●

Focus_____**Date/Time** _____

Stretch ◯   **Warm-Up** _____

Strength/Balance/Flexibility Training

Exercise		Set 1	Set 2	Set 3	Set 4	Set 5
	Reps					
	Weight					
	Reps					
	Weight					
	Reps					
	Weight					
	Reps					
	Weight					
	Reps					
	Weight					
	Reps					
	Weight					
	Reps					
	Weight					
	Reps					
	Weight					
	Reps					
	Weight					
	Reps					
	Weight					

Cardio

Exercise	Calories	Distance	Time

Water Intake _____

Cooldown _____

Feeling ☆ ☆ ☆ ☆ ☆

Notes

_____
_____

Today's Goal _____   (M) (T) (W) (T) (F) (S) (S)

Focus_____**Date/Time** _____

Stretch ○   **Warm-Up** _____

Strength/Balance/Flexibility Training

Exercise		Set 1	Set 2	Set 3	Set 4	Set 5
	Reps					
	Weight					
	Reps					
	Weight					
	Reps					
	Weight					
	Reps					
	Weight					
	Reps					
	Weight					
	Reps					
	Weight					
	Reps					
	Weight					
	Reps					
	Weight					
	Reps					
	Weight					
	Reps					
	Weight					

Cardio

Exercise	Calories	Distance	Time

Water Intake _____

Cooldown _____

Feeling ☆ ☆ ☆ ☆ ☆

Notes

Today's Goal _____ Ⓜ Ⓣ Ⓦ Ⓣ Ⓕ ⬤ ⬤

Focus_____Date/Time _____

Stretch ◯   Warm-Up _____

Strength/Balance/Flexibility Training

Exercise		Set 1	Set 2	Set 3	Set 4	Set 5
	Reps					
	Weight					
	Reps					
	Weight					
	Reps					
	Weight					
	Reps					
	Weight					
	Reps					
	Weight					
	Reps					
	Weight					
	Reps					
	Weight					
	Reps					
	Weight					
	Reps					
	Weight					
	Reps					
	Weight					

Cardio

Exercise	Calories	Distance	Time

Water Intake _____

Cooldown _____

Feeling ☆ ☆ ☆ ☆ ☆

Notes

Today's Goal _____ Ⓜ Ⓣ Ⓦ Ⓣ Ⓕ ⬤ ⬤

Focus_____**Date/Time** _____

Stretch ◯   **Warm-Up** _____

Strength/Balance/Flexibility Training

Exercise		Set 1	Set 2	Set 3	Set 4	Set 5
	Reps					
	Weight					
	Reps					
	Weight					
	Reps					
	Weight					
	Reps					
	Weight					
	Reps					
	Weight					
	Reps					
	Weight					
	Reps					
	Weight					
	Reps					
	Weight					
	Reps					
	Weight					
	Reps					
	Weight					

Cardio

Exercise	Calories	Distance	Time

Water Intake _____

Cooldown _____

Feeling ☆ ☆ ☆ ☆ ☆

Notes

Today's Goal _____ Ⓜ Ⓣ Ⓦ Ⓣ Ⓕ ⬤ ⬤

Focus _____ **Date/Time** _____

Stretch ◯ **Warm-Up** _____

Strength/Balance/Flexibility Training

Exercise		Set 1	Set 2	Set 3	Set 4	Set 5
	Reps					
	Weight					
	Reps					
	Weight					
	Reps					
	Weight					
	Reps					
	Weight					
	Reps					
	Weight					
	Reps					
	Weight					
	Reps					
	Weight					
	Reps					
	Weight					
	Reps					
	Weight					
	Reps					
	Weight					

Cardio

Exercise	Calories	Distance	Time

Water Intake _____

Cooldown _____

Feeling ☆ ☆ ☆ ☆ ☆

Notes

Today's Goal _____

(M) (T) (W) (T) (F) (S) (S)

Focus_____ Date/Time _____

Stretch ◯   Warm-Up _____

Strength/Balance/Flexibility Training

Exercise		Set 1	Set 2	Set 3	Set 4	Set 5
	Reps					
	Weight					
	Reps					
	Weight					
	Reps					
	Weight					
	Reps					
	Weight					
	Reps					
	Weight					
	Reps					
	Weight					
	Reps					
	Weight					
	Reps					
	Weight					
	Reps					
	Weight					
	Reps					
	Weight					

Cardio

Exercise	Calories	Distance	Time

Water Intake _____

Cooldown _____

Feeling ☆ ☆ ☆ ☆ ☆

Notes

Today's Goal _____   (M) (T) (W) (T) (F) (S) (S)

Focus_____**Date/Time** _____

Stretch ◯   **Warm-Up** _____

Strength/Balance/Flexibility Training

Exercise		Set 1	Set 2	Set 3	Set 4	Set 5
	Reps					
	Weight					
	Reps					
	Weight					
	Reps					
	Weight					
	Reps					
	Weight					
	Reps					
	Weight					
	Reps					
	Weight					
	Reps					
	Weight					
	Reps					
	Weight					
	Reps					
	Weight					
	Reps					
	Weight					

Cardio

Exercise	Calories	Distance	Time

Water Intake _____

Cooldown _____

Feeling ☆ ☆ ☆ ☆ ☆

Notes

Today's Goal _____   Ⓜ Ⓣ Ⓦ Ⓣ Ⓕ ⬤ ⬤

Focus_____**Date/Time** _____

Stretch ◯   **Warm-Up** _____

Strength/Balance/Flexibility Training

Exercise		Set 1	Set 2	Set 3	Set 4	Set 5
	Reps					
	Weight					
	Reps					
	Weight					
	Reps					
	Weight					
	Reps					
	Weight					
	Reps					
	Weight					
	Reps					
	Weight					
	Reps					
	Weight					
	Reps					
	Weight					
	Reps					
	Weight					
	Reps					
	Weight					

Cardio

Exercise	Calories	Distance	Time

Water Intake _____

Cooldown _____

Feeling ☆ ☆ ☆ ☆ ☆

Notes

Today's Goal _____ Ⓜ Ⓣ Ⓦ Ⓣ Ⓕ ⬤ ⬤

Focus_____**Date/Time** _____

Stretch ◯   **Warm-Up** _____

Strength/Balance/Flexibility Training

Exercise		Set 1	Set 2	Set 3	Set 4	Set 5
	Reps					
	Weight					
	Reps					
	Weight					
	Reps					
	Weight					
	Reps					
	Weight					
	Reps					
	Weight					
	Reps					
	Weight					
	Reps					
	Weight					
	Reps					
	Weight					
	Reps					
	Weight					
	Reps					
	Weight					

Cardio

Exercise	Calories	Distance	Time

Water Intake _____

Cooldown _____

Feeling ☆ ☆ ☆ ☆ ☆

Notes

Today's Goal _____ Ⓜ Ⓣ Ⓦ Ⓣ Ⓕ ⬤ ⬤

Focus_____**Date/Time**_____

Stretch ◯   **Warm-Up** _____

Strength/Balance/Flexibility Training

Exercise		Set 1	Set 2	Set 3	Set 4	Set 5
	Reps					
	Weight					
	Reps					
	Weight					
	Reps					
	Weight					
	Reps					
	Weight					
	Reps					
	Weight					
	Reps					
	Weight					
	Reps					
	Weight					
	Reps					
	Weight					
	Reps					
	Weight					
	Reps					
	Weight					

Cardio

Exercise	Calories	Distance	Time

Water Intake _____

Cooldown _____

Feeling ☆ ☆ ☆ ☆ ☆

Notes

Today's Goal _____ Ⓜ Ⓣ Ⓦ Ⓣ Ⓕ ⬤ ⬤

Focus_____**Date/Time** _____

Stretch ◯   **Warm-Up** _____

Strength/Balance/Flexibility Training

Exercise		Set 1	Set 2	Set 3	Set 4	Set 5
	Reps					
	Weight					
	Reps					
	Weight					
	Reps					
	Weight					
	Reps					
	Weight					
	Reps					
	Weight					
	Reps					
	Weight					
	Reps					
	Weight					
	Reps					
	Weight					
	Reps					
	Weight					
	Reps					
	Weight					

Cardio

Exercise	Calories	Distance	Time

Water Intake _____

Cooldown _____

Feeling ☆ ☆ ☆ ☆ ☆

Notes

Today's Goal _____

(M) (T) (W) (T) (F) (S) (S)

Focus_____ **Date/Time** _____

Stretch ◯   **Warm-Up** _____

Strength/Balance/Flexibility Training

Exercise		Set 1	Set 2	Set 3	Set 4	Set 5
	Reps					
	Weight					
	Reps					
	Weight					
	Reps					
	Weight					
	Reps					
	Weight					
	Reps					
	Weight					
	Reps					
	Weight					
	Reps					
	Weight					
	Reps					
	Weight					
	Reps					
	Weight					
	Reps					
	Weight					

Cardio

Exercise	Calories	Distance	Time

Water Intake _____

Cooldown _____

Feeling ☆ ☆ ☆ ☆ ☆

Notes

Today's Goal _____ Ⓜ Ⓣ Ⓦ Ⓣ Ⓕ 🅂 🅂

Focus_____ Date/Time _____

Stretch ◯   Warm-Up _____

Strength/Balance/Flexibility Training

Exercise		Set 1	Set 2	Set 3	Set 4	Set 5
	Reps					
	Weight					
	Reps					
	Weight					
	Reps					
	Weight					
	Reps					
	Weight					
	Reps					
	Weight					
	Reps					
	Weight					
	Reps					
	Weight					
	Reps					
	Weight					
	Reps					
	Weight					
	Reps					
	Weight					

Cardio

Exercise	Calories	Distance	Time

Water Intake _____

Cooldown _____

Feeling ☆ ☆ ☆ ☆ ☆

Notes

Today's Goal _____ (M) (T) (W) (T) (F) **S** **S**

Focus_____Date/Time _____

Stretch ◯   Warm-Up _____

Strength/Balance/Flexibility Training

Exercise		Set 1	Set 2	Set 3	Set 4	Set 5
	Reps					
	Weight					
	Reps					
	Weight					
	Reps					
	Weight					
	Reps					
	Weight					
	Reps					
	Weight					
	Reps					
	Weight					
	Reps					
	Weight					
	Reps					
	Weight					
	Reps					
	Weight					
	Reps					
	Weight					

Cardio

Exercise	Calories	Distance	Time

Water Intake _____

Cooldown _____

Feeling ☆ ☆ ☆ ☆ ☆

Notes

Today's Goal _____ Ⓜ Ⓣ Ⓦ Ⓣ Ⓕ ⬤ ⬤

Focus_____**Date/Time** _____

Stretch ◯   **Warm-Up** _____

Strength/Balance/Flexibility Training

Exercise		Set 1	Set 2	Set 3	Set 4	Set 5
	Reps					
	Weight					
	Reps					
	Weight					
	Reps					
	Weight					
	Reps					
	Weight					
	Reps					
	Weight					
	Reps					
	Weight					
	Reps					
	Weight					
	Reps					
	Weight					
	Reps					
	Weight					
	Reps					
	Weight					

Cardio

Exercise	Calories	Distance	Time

Water Intake _____

Cooldown _____

Feeling ☆ ☆ ☆ ☆ ☆

Notes

Today's Goal _____ Ⓜ Ⓣ Ⓦ Ⓣ Ⓕ Ⓢ Ⓢ

Focus_____**Date/Time** _____

Stretch ◯   **Warm-Up** _____

Strength/Balance/Flexibility Training

Exercise		Set 1	Set 2	Set 3	Set 4	Set 5
	Reps					
	Weight					
	Reps					
	Weight					
	Reps					
	Weight					
	Reps					
	Weight					
	Reps					
	Weight					
	Reps					
	Weight					
	Reps					
	Weight					
	Reps					
	Weight					
	Reps					
	Weight					
	Reps					
	Weight					

Cardio

Exercise	Calories	Distance	Time

Water Intake _____

Cooldown _____

Feeling ☆ ☆ ☆ ☆ ☆

Notes

Today's Goal _____ Ⓜ Ⓣ Ⓦ Ⓣ Ⓕ ⬤ ⬤

Focus_____**Date/Time** _____

Stretch ◯   **Warm-Up** _____

Strength/Balance/Flexibility Training

Exercise		Set 1	Set 2	Set 3	Set 4	Set 5
	Reps					
	Weight					
	Reps					
	Weight					
	Reps					
	Weight					
	Reps					
	Weight					
	Reps					
	Weight					
	Reps					
	Weight					
	Reps					
	Weight					
	Reps					
	Weight					
	Reps					
	Weight					
	Reps					
	Weight					

Cardio

Exercise	Calories	Distance	Time

Water Intake _____

Cooldown _____

Feeling ☆ ☆ ☆ ☆ ☆

Notes

Today's Goal _____ Ⓜ Ⓣ Ⓦ Ⓣ Ⓕ 🄂 🄂

Focus_____**Date/Time** _____

Stretch ◯   **Warm-Up** _____

Strength/Balance/Flexibility Training

Exercise		Set 1	Set 2	Set 3	Set 4	Set 5
	Reps					
	Weight					
	Reps					
	Weight					
	Reps					
	Weight					
	Reps					
	Weight					
	Reps					
	Weight					
	Reps					
	Weight					
	Reps					
	Weight					
	Reps					
	Weight					
	Reps					
	Weight					
	Reps					
	Weight					

Cardio

Exercise	Calories	Distance	Time

Water Intake _____

Cooldown _____

Feeling ☆ ☆ ☆ ☆ ☆

Notes

Today's Goal _____ Ⓜ Ⓣ Ⓦ Ⓣ Ⓕ ⬤ ⬤

Focus_____**Date/Time** _____

Stretch ◯   **Warm-Up** _____

Strength/Balance/Flexibility Training

Exercise		Set 1	Set 2	Set 3	Set 4	Set 5
	Reps					
	Weight					
	Reps					
	Weight					
	Reps					
	Weight					
	Reps					
	Weight					
	Reps					
	Weight					
	Reps					
	Weight					
	Reps					
	Weight					
	Reps					
	Weight					
	Reps					
	Weight					
	Reps					
	Weight					

Cardio

Exercise	Calories	Distance	Time

Water Intake _____

Cooldown _____

Feeling ☆ ☆ ☆ ☆ ☆

Notes

Today's Goal _____ Ⓜ Ⓣ Ⓦ Ⓣ Ⓕ ⬤ ⬤

Focus_____**Date/Time** _____

Stretch ◯   **Warm-Up** _____

Strength/Balance/Flexibility Training

Exercise		Set 1	Set 2	Set 3	Set 4	Set 5
	Reps					
	Weight					
	Reps					
	Weight					
	Reps					
	Weight					
	Reps					
	Weight					
	Reps					
	Weight					
	Reps					
	Weight					
	Reps					
	Weight					
	Reps					
	Weight					
	Reps					
	Weight					
	Reps					
	Weight					

Cardio

Exercise	Calories	Distance	Time

Water Intake _____

Cooldown _____

Feeling ☆ ☆ ☆ ☆ ☆

Notes

Today's Goal _____   (M) (T) (W) (T) (F) (S) (S)

Focus _____ **Date/Time** _____

Stretch ◯   **Warm-Up** _____

Strength/Balance/Flexibility Training

Exercise		Set 1	Set 2	Set 3	Set 4	Set 5
	Reps					
	Weight					
	Reps					
	Weight					
	Reps					
	Weight					
	Reps					
	Weight					
	Reps					
	Weight					
	Reps					
	Weight					
	Reps					
	Weight					
	Reps					
	Weight					
	Reps					
	Weight					
	Reps					
	Weight					

Cardio

Exercise	Calories	Distance	Time

Water Intake _____

Cooldown _____

Feeling ☆ ☆ ☆ ☆ ☆

Notes

Today's Goal _____ Ⓜ Ⓣ Ⓦ Ⓣ Ⓕ ⬤ ⬤

Focus_____Date/Time _____

Stretch ◯   Warm-Up _____

Strength/Balance/Flexibility Training

Exercise		Set 1	Set 2	Set 3	Set 4	Set 5
	Reps					
	Weight					
	Reps					
	Weight					
	Reps					
	Weight					
	Reps					
	Weight					
	Reps					
	Weight					
	Reps					
	Weight					
	Reps					
	Weight					
	Reps					
	Weight					
	Reps					
	Weight					
	Reps					
	Weight					

Cardio

Exercise	Calories	Distance	Time

Water Intake _____

Cooldown _____

Feeling ☆ ☆ ☆ ☆ ☆

Notes

Today's Goal _____

(M) (T) (W) (T) (F) (S) (S)

Focus_____ **Date/Time** _____

Stretch ◯   **Warm-Up** _____

Strength/Balance/Flexibility Training

Exercise		Set 1	Set 2	Set 3	Set 4	Set 5
	Reps					
	Weight					
	Reps					
	Weight					
	Reps					
	Weight					
	Reps					
	Weight					
	Reps					
	Weight					
	Reps					
	Weight					
	Reps					
	Weight					
	Reps					
	Weight					
	Reps					
	Weight					
	Reps					
	Weight					
	Reps					
	Weight					
	Reps					
	Weight					

Cardio

Exercise	Calories	Distance	Time

Water Intake _____

Cooldown _____

Feeling ☆ ☆ ☆ ☆ ☆

Notes

Made in the USA
Columbia, SC
02 December 2024

48304182R00093